SUCCESSFUL SEMINAR SELLING

If you want to know how...

Getting Free Publicity
Secrets of successful press relations

100 Ways to Make Your Business a Success
A resource book for small businesses

Marketing for Complementary Therapists
101 tried and tested ways to attract clients

Starting Your Own Business
The bestselling guide to planning and building a successful enterprise

SUCCESSFUL SEMINAR SELLING

The ultimate small business guide to boosting sales and profits through seminars and workshops

Philip Calvert

howtobooks

To Sarah, Tom, Isobel and Ben. This is for you.

To those with the power to inspire:
Denis Waitley, Allan Pease and Ted Nugent
for lighting the fire.

Thanks also to everyone who has helped, encouraged
or made a contribution, particularly:
Sarah for help and support well beyond the call of duty, Nikki Read, Digby Jones, Roland Rawicz-Szczerbo, Jacqui Smith, Tony Raynor, Alan Bell, Big John,
Baloo the Bear, Deborah Hall, Marie Mosely, Rikki Arundel, Roy Sheppard,
Nolan D. Archibald, Jacqui Harper and
David Calvert for his superb photography.

Published by How To Books Ltd,
3 Newtec Place, Magdalen Road,
Oxford OX4 1RE. United Kingdom.
Tel: (01865) 793806. Fax: (01865) 248780.
email: info@howtobooks.co.uk
http://www.howtobooks.co.uk

British Library Cataloguing in Publication Data
A catalogue record for this book is available from the British Library

Edited by Diana Brueton
Cover design by Baseline Arts Ltd, Oxford
Produced for How To Books by Deer Park Productions, Tavistock
Typeset by PDQ Typesetting, Newcastle-under-Lyme, Staffs.
Printed and bound in Great Britain by Bell & Bain Ltd, Glasgow

Contents

Part 3 What Happens Next?

About the author

Philip Calvert is a professional speaker and recognised expert in Seminar Selling and Internet Marketing – providing entertaining, informative, dynamic keynote speeches and powerful, educational workshops. If you have ever attended Phil's unique whole day workshop 'The Secrets of Successful Seminar Selling' you will know that he is a speaker with a passion for inspiring audiences, individuals and small businesses to raise their game and achieve challenging goals.

> 'My own inspiration comes from artists in the world of rock music, where enthusiasm, energy and commitment is a given. Whilst music is their art, it is also their business – and without that magical mixture of creativity, passion, drive and live performance many would fade into obscurity. Small business owners are also passionate about what they do and those willing to take their business message to clients and customers through seminars, workshops and live demonstrations will see incredible results.'

Founder and owner of Training Strategies Limited, Phil advises business owners, senior executives and sales professionals on advanced presentation skills techniques and how to maximise profits through Seminar Selling and Internet Marketing.

Introduction

In this book owners of small businesses will discover a proactive, exciting, profitable and proven formula for increasing sales.

I am a huge believer in the commonsense notion that the amount of effort you put into your business determines the results you get out of it. It hopefully follows that if you positively and proactively set about increasing sales, you will be rewarded with strong results.

But some ways of increasing sales are much more effective than others and this book reveals the secrets behind just one – one which offers potentially the greatest returns. And whilst the book is aimed at small businesses, the techniques and ideas included can equally apply to larger organisations and their sales people.

Seminar Selling is not a new idea and many people will have participated in a seminar at some stage in their career. Very few, however, continue with this marketing approach for a number of reasons – be it fear of public speaking, concern at the amount of organisation involved, the cost of holding the events or even lack of awareness of the potential benefits. This book will show you specifically:

- Why Seminar Selling can be key to significant growth and profits.
- The (considerable) benefits available to *all* small businesses – not just white-collar sectors.
- The benefits to attendees of your seminars.
- How to plan, prepare, market and host your seminars.
- The special presentation skills needed to deliver your business messages with power, clarity, confidence, conviction and impact.
- How to follow up afterwards.
- Extra ideas to help you maximise profits.

For those prepared to master the skills and 'get on with it', the results can be astonishing. In fact, business people who do use seminars as part of their sales strategy generally swear by the approach. Andrew Brown is an independent financial adviser in Weston-super-Mare and is one of those people. I am extremely grateful to him for his fantastic contribution.

Seminar Selling is all about getting on your feet and demonstrating your expertise – live! It's up close and personal and the audience can see the whites of your eyes. It takes guts, hard work, passion, energy and commitment. But get it right and you will never look back. This book removes much of the hard work by revealing everything you need to know to successfully plan, prepare and host your seminars – including the special presentation skills needed to get your business message across with clarity, confidence and conviction.

And here's even better news.

The advent of the internet and new communication technology now provides the opportunity to not only promote your seminars, but to be integrated into your sales and service proposition in a way that will skyrocket your profits. Seminar Selling today is about the skilful combination of a variety of traditional and modern sales and marketing techniques and I hope this book will empower you to discover an exciting, creative, proactive and incredibly profitable new direction for your business.

Throughout the book I refer to 'your seminars' or 'your workshops', which to some readers might imply a formal, intellectual meeting, debate or discussion. I use these words to generically mean *any public event* which you might put on to demonstrate an aspect of your business, service or expertise – regardless of the nature of your business. It could be a wine tasting, a craft demonstration or a workshop on how to plan for your retirement. Whatever it is, this book will give you exciting new ideas on how to promote your business more effectively than ever before.

Also revealed in the book are a number of fantastic marketing tips, tricks and secrets which I have picked up over the years. Some work for me and others don't, but I wanted to include everything that could potentially be of value to the reader. Where I know the source of a particular idea I have included it. There are others though which I have attempted to source, but which unfortunately remain part of sales and marketing folklore. If you know the source of any references please let me know.

Part 1

Successful Seminar Selling: How To Plan, Prepare and Market Your Events

1

Problems Facing Small Businesses

'Change' is a wonderful thing. It keeps life fresh and exciting and brings a wealth of opportunity for anyone who is prepared to grasp it. *'You're either on the train – or under it'* as a colleague once helpfully advised me.

On the other hand, a great many business people don't see it that way. Change brings fear, worry, uncertainty and indecision, which isn't surprising if you are to believe the business editorials of the weekend press, each proclaiming the results of survey after survey on the worries of small businesses. In fact, you would be forgiven for wondering why anyone actually starts their own business.

A recent survey from NatWest Bank revealed the main concerns. These included:

- the changing economic climate
- cash flow/late payment of bills
- changing regulations
- changing European law
- lack of skilled employees
- the minimum wage
- competition
- the overall tax burden
- changing exchange rates
- cost of transport
- postal problems
- the price of bottled water

...and so on.

I made up the last one, but it does seem as if small businesses in some industries just aren't happy unless they are worrying about something.

But in all seriousness, the small business owner does have much to contend with on a day-to-day basis. And one thing is for certain: change will continue for many years to come. Not only will it continue, but it will *confuse* as it continues. Take marketing for example.

Changing technology now gives the small business owner an extraordinary array of promotional tools and methodologies. Here are just a few:

- telesales
- face to face sales
- fax marketing
- direct mail
- TV advertising
- radio advertising
- newspaper advertising
- magazine advertising
- internet marketing
- affinity marketing
- email marketing
- key account management
- relationship management
- text messaging.

And as we'll discover later – yes, even advertising on the side of sheep!

So surely the degree to which we can adapt to change will determine our ability to profit from it and is the key to moving forward in our business. Unfortunately, in the UK we are often slow in recognising when change has happened and by the time we have decided to take advantage of, say, some new technological advance, many of the potential new benefits have often been lost. As we will see shortly, less than 10% of British small businesses are using the internet regularly to build sales. Most *think* they are, but believe me, they're not! Simply having a website does not necessarily mean we are maximising the potential from e-commerce.

In the United States many, many people have completely reengineered their businesses to take advantage of the potential from e-commerce, yet in the UK we tend to see the internet as just another promotional tool (that we don't yet fully understand). Some readers may feel that their business sector or product is not appropriate for online sales and that's fair enough, but later on I will show other ways in which you can use your website to generate substantial new sales.

So how does the average small business owner look beyond all the distractions of change, European law, exchange rates, stealth taxes and late payments and get focused on producing volume, profitable sales? After all, the Federation of Small Business' (FSB) report *Lifting the Barriers to Growth in UK Small Businesses 2002* reveals that moderate or substantial growth is a key goal for the majority of small businesses in the UK. Good news!

According to the same survey, the small business' most favoured methods of achieving that growth are to:

- increase turnover
- increase profits
- engage in new ventures and
- improve marketing.

'Improve marketing'. Even better!

But the factor believed to be most important to survival and growth was their own business' capabilities, i.e. the strength and robustness of their core product and service proposition.

But then there's the problem of funding.

FUNDING FOR GROWTH

Funding any growth programme is inevitably going to be a challenge for all small businesses and whilst there are numerous government initiatives and grants available, these resources are not without limit. A clear majority of small businesses resort to bank overdrafts to sustain and grow their organisations, which is of course absurdly expensive – even in today's low interest rate environment.

How then is it possible for a small business (or any other business for that matter) to respond positively to change, engage proactively in new ventures, increase turnover, improve marketing *and* achieve significant growth all at the same time and without breaking the bank?

A tough question for any business, let alone firms that operate within sectors that are undergoing *additional* change and consolidation, like financial services for example.

Some commentators have suggested that eventually technology will revolutionise everything – and this may well be the case, but with the exception of predominantly research and operational functions, internet technologies are simply not being used by small businesses to increase sales to any significant extent. The FSB survey reports that its respondents were most likely to use internet services to send emails, transfer files and documents or gather information. *Only 6% regularly used the internet to review business opportunities or bid for work and only 9% regularly used it for e-commerce purposes.*

So use of the internet to help achieve their growth goals is some way off, but there are ways it can be used to support other initiatives which will themselves produce high levels of new business and we will explore some of these later in this book.

The FSB Survey also reveals other factors that are perceived by small businesses as important to business survival and growth:

- finance and banking (55%)
- the ability to employ staff (55%)
- legislation (46%)
- business advice (46%)
- transport (45%)
- education and training (40%)
- government funded business support (27%)
- public services (27%)
- EU funding and funded programmes (20%).

No great surprises here, though it's disappointing to see that education and training is not considered *more* important to business survival and growth. Even more disappointing is that a category for sales and marketing is not highlighted in its own right.

Furthermore, there are some basic sales and marketing issues that are vital to business survival and growth. With everything else to think about, it's easy to forget them:

- You need a regular supply of new and existing customers.
- These customers need to trust you.
- You need to understand them intimately – this includes understanding their problems.
- You need a product or service that solves these problems.
- You need a service proposition that gives prospects and customers slightly more than they expect. This means treating them in ways that will make them loyal customers for life and not treating them how you *think* they want to be treated or how you think they *should* be treated.
- Potential customers need evidence of your expertise and, ideally, third party endorsement of your product or service.
- Once potential customers have found you, they must find your product or service irresistible.
- You need to do it all profitably.

Boiled down further these sales and marketing 'business basics' equate to a need for:

- Proactive marketing.
- Exceptional creativity skills.
- An extremely thorough understanding of customers' needs.

- Credibility in business.
- The provision of considerable 'added value' through customer service.

In the next chapter we will look at the one and only way that small businesses can incorporate all these 'business basics' within their marketing strategy, proactively move forward whilst increasing sales and profits *and* all within the context of a dramatically changing and often highly regulated business environment.

An impossible dream? Read on.

2

The Need to Change and Adapt

'The most important thing a small business can do is be clear about what their end game is, be specific about the target market and then prepare a marketing plan covering at least 12 months' activity.

The marketing plan should explore different marketing approaches from direct response mailings, advertising, PR and affinity relationships. They must set up a program of measuring every return from every campaign so that the most effective marketing strategy can be identified. Once they have found something that works, then they should keep on using the approach until it begins to falter. Once this happens they need to try again with a different approach.

The marketing message must always be benefit driven and focused on the end user and not the business. No one is interested about how great I think my business is – all I want to know is how you are going to help me. WIIFM (What's in it for me?) is all a target cares about.

Having started the marketing process it is vital that you stick with it. Far too often a novice will expect immediate returns from their marketing effort – it never happens. Keep refining the marketing messages (from the prospect's perspective), test different headlines that grab the attention, make sure that headline claims are substantiated in the text, explain how the client will benefit if they use your service or buy your product and also what they will lose out on if they don't. Have a powerful call for action and offer some sort of guarantee that ensures the client will never lose out if they find that the product is not what they want. (Risk reversal is powerful so long as you are confident in your product or service). Finally, use special offers to grab the attention and heighten the sense of loss if they fail to take action.

Roland Rawicz-Szczerbo, Director,
Quay Software Solutions Limited

Any small business owner wishing or needing to proactively move forward, with a view to dramatically increasing sales, requires a great deal of self-motivation and courage – not to mention creative and lateral thinking.

Even if you are an expert in a particular field and have produced a good living from your business, it is very easy to become blinkered in your approach to sales and marketing. If a particular sales approach has worked well enough up until now, then why bother to change it? But is that what you really want?

Ask yourself a few questions:

- Is your current sales approach producing sufficient *new* business for you?
- Is it maximising full sales potential?
- Would you like to be selling *more* of your product or service?
- Do you run the risk of this method running out of steam in time?
- Have you thought about new ways of increasing sales to meet the changing needs of customers?

Whatever your answers to these questions, it's vital that you still keep an open mind to a wide variety of new ways of building sales – even if you truly believe you have found the one and only way for your business. Ask yourself this: Is it possible that there might just be a better, more efficient and more cost effective way of promoting your product or service? My challenge and bet with you is that there is.

THINKING LATERALLY

First of all, let's explore lateral thinking a bit more. Much has been written about the need for lateral thinking and I don't intend to add a great deal more here. But what is often forgotten is just how hard it is to think laterally.

'Think laterally' we are told on one course after another, as if by magic we can suddenly conjure up exciting new ways to achieve our goals. It just doesn't work like that. What *is* possible though is for business owners to be much more open minded about how they approach problems and opportunities. In businesses of all sizes, we are not very good at this.

> 'We tried that five years ago and it didn't work (so it won't work now).'
> 'Clients don't buy our sort of products off the internet.'
> 'Radio advertising wouldn't be right for us.'
> 'We're not salespeople – we provide advice.'

You know the sort of thing.

As a result, we stick to the same old ways of doing things in the vain hope that business will improve on its own accord and our minds remain firmly closed to new opportunities and new ways of promoting and delivering our products and services.

Try this little test.

Write down the next four numbers in this sequence. (If you can get the next six, give yourself a pat on the back!)

3 1 2 8 3 1 3 0 . . .

Unless you can see the answer straight away, I can bet that you have approached the problem in much the same way that you always have – by looking for some sort of mathematical formula or pattern. Memories of school maths lessons come flooding back as your mind searches for the link between each number. And that is, of course, the issue. We're approaching the problem in exactly the same way that we always have. Wouldn't it be great if we had the ability to 'think laterally' at the switch of a button?!

Now look at the numbers again, but open your mind to different possibilities and solutions.

3 1 2 8 3 1 3 0 . . .

That's enough clues. If you think you know the answer, send an email to solution@trainingstrategies.co.uk

One way that we could open our minds just a little bit would be to not make assumptions about how customers and prospects want to receive information or use technology. For example, there is a perception amongst many people that the Internet is not likely to be used to any great extent by 'older people'. Not only is it used, but according to research undertaken by ICM for Age Concern in July 2002, two-thirds of IT users over the age of 55 agreed that the internet had a positive impact on their lives.

IT users over the age of 55 also used the internet to:

- contact family and friends in the UK (82%)
- investigate websites about hobbies (72%)
- contact family and friends abroad (66%)
- manage their bank account (34%)
- research flights/holidays (67%)
- check the news (41%)
- check financial issues (39%)
- search for local information (45%)
- research family history (26%).

Given information like this, isn't it about time we started to take notice of reports that the 'grey market' is growing at an astonishing rate and shouldn't we now be updating our perception of how older consumers like to obtain their information?

I enjoy stirring things up a bit when I meet representatives from different industries who feel that their particular sector is quite advanced in its use of technology. Indeed, many are very advanced when it comes to technology for operational purposes, but many have a long way to go to make full use of the potential it offers to increase sales.

'Do you think that independent financial advisers (IFAs) are ready for bulk text messaging?' I asked an industry marketing figure recently.

'Not quite' came the rather respectful reply. Again making an assumption based on perception rather than fact. Little did he know that during the same week a colleague and I had experimented by sending follow-up text messages to a group of IFAs after a presentation we had given. In short, we were astonished by the positive responses we received and will be repeating the exercise.

The same ICM survey for Age Concern also revealed some interesting figures about the use of text messaging facilities amongst older people – a group of people one might be tempted to assume would not normally be associated with this relatively new form of communication. Interestingly, nearly a quarter of all respondents over the age of 55 used the text facility, rising to 34% amongst those who already use a computer. And don't I know it – my 68-year-old mother-in-law is a big fan of text messaging to 'keep in touch'.

In conclusion, I firmly believe that as business people we make far too many assumptions about how customers want to receive information and spend too little time investigating new ways of making our sales and marketing efforts more innovative or efficient. As a result we are missing out on huge new opportunities, both at home and abroad. To some extent this is understandable, perhaps for no other reason than the fact that if our current sales and marketing methodology ain't apparently broke, then there's no need to fix it. But as the FSB survey told us, moderate or substantial growth is still a key goal for the majority of small businesses in the UK.

Fear of change and fear that a new approach won't work is a natural inhibiting factor for most businesses. So, wouldn't it be great if we could find an approach to sales and marketing which is not only tried, tested and proven, but also new, profitable, exciting, creative and innovative for most small businesses?

3

The Benefits of Seminar Selling

'A good idea is not enough to make a business work. Successful entrepreneurs have a knack for exploiting ideas and turning them into commercial reality.

Make sure you have identified a market need and that they are aware of your solution. Without promotion, no one will know your idea exists.'

Digby Jones, Director-General,
Confederation of British Industry (CBI)

Remember our 'business basics' from the first chapter?

- You need regular communication with both new and existing customers – and they need to trust you.
- You need to understand them and their problems intimately and have a product or service which solves these problems.
- You need a service proposition that gives prospects and customers more than they expect. This means treating them in ways that will make them loyal customers for life and not treating them how you *think* they want to be treated or how you think they *should* be treated.
- Potential customers need evidence of your expertise and, ideally, third party endorsement of your product/service. Once you are in contact with potential customers, they must find your product and service irresistible.
- You need to do it all profitably.

Boiled down further these business basics equate to a need for:

- Proactive marketing.
- Exceptional creativity skills.
- An extremely thorough understanding of customers' needs.
- Credibility in business.
- The provision of considerable 'added value' through outstanding customer service.

In my view, Seminar Selling is the only real way of promoting your product and service in a way that encapsulates all of these business basics at the same time *and* which enables small businesses on a tight marketing budget to achieve significant increases in sales and profitable growth.

There is a perception though, that Seminar Selling is just for white-collar businesses, so it is important to stress at this point that virtually *any small business* can profit significantly – particularly if you have products or services that benefit from demonstration to explain how they work. In fact, it may well be the case that your product or service may gain more than you realise from a live demonstration.

WHAT IS SEMINAR SELLING?

Earl Tupper's plastic consumer products were a revolution in the kitchen when they were first introduced in 1946. But despite their many advantages, they did not sell very well in retail outlets. So it was decided that the unique advantages of the plastic containers needed demonstrating to help consumers to understand how they worked and to appreciate the key benefits. The first Tupperware Home Party was held in 1948 with the demonstrations proving incredibly successful – so much so that in 1951, Tupperware products were removed from retail outlets.

The rest, as they say, is history, but it is interesting to note how the company has adapted and modified its sales approach to cater for changes in society and shopping preferences. In 1992, the company introduced Custom Kitchen Planning demonstrations where customers could learn about food preparation, microwave cooking and ways to save money on their grocery bills. Today, the company is making full use of the internet and also demonstrations and showcases in shopping centres. In short, Tupperware are superb exponents of Seminar or Workshop Selling.

Most of us have attended a seminar, workshop or demonstration at some stage in our lives. Our prime motivation was probably to obtain information on a subject in which we had an interest. It could have been a hobby, or perhaps we wanted more detailed information on a product or service prior to making a major purchase. We may even have attended a 'party selling' event promoting anything from kitchenware, lingerie, jewellery, water purification products, security systems, diet plans, cleaning products, cosmetics, children's books or crafts. And on occasion we will have been given an incentive to attend, such as free flights, a mountain bike, a wide screen television or maybe £10,000 cash!

But for the most part, it was the *content* of the seminar or workshop that was the influencing factor and which had the potential to further boost our interest in a subject, product or service. And that is the secret of successful Seminar Selling – *the ability to inspire attendees to come back for more – much more.*

We could just as easily have requested a brochure from the company concerned, or perhaps looked at their website. We could even have asked for a representative to come to our house. But a seminar is different. Not only are we able to gain much more information than through a brochure or a website, but it gives us an insight into the workings and culture of the company and its people, affording us a glimpse 'behind the scenes' prior to committing ourselves further. And some products simply sell better from the benefit of a demonstration.

As I explained earlier, Seminar Selling encapsulates all our business basics, giving us a platform to promote and demonstrate the services of our business and allows potential customers to experience us and our product in a 'live' environment without pressure, thus enabling a relationship and trust to develop.

Your 'seminar' can be anything from a full day, flashy, professional, multi-media presentation in a smart hotel or conference venue, to a simple 'how to' demonstration or workshop in your shop, office premises or home. Without realising it, you may already give demonstrations to potential clients or customers and there's a good chance that you yourself have been influenced to make purchases as a result of seeing a demonstration. It happens everywhere without you even noticing – for example, department stores that give cosmetic and make-up demonstrations; wine merchants and off-licences offering free tastings; kitchen and house ware demonstrations at county fairs.

The purpose of this book is to show you how to harness the considerable benefits of promoting your products and services at seminars and workshops and to give you the confidence and skills to transfer these benefits to your own business.

How Seminar Selling works

I witnessed a superb example of this when I was speaking recently at a Women in Enterprise event in South Wales, where a young lady was welcomed as a new member to the group. Without realising she had done it, Nadine provided the best possible example of Seminar Selling in action.

Nadine was in the process of starting her new business as a Colour and Image Consultant, showing clients, predominantly women, how to discover and enhance the best aspects of their appearance and how to choose clothing and accessories of the correct colour for their skin and hair tones. During her ten-minute presentation to introduce herself (her first ever 'stand up' presentation) she demonstrated her colour analysis technique by holding swatches of different coloured material under the faces of two female volunteers from the audience.

It was clear to anyone that volunteer number one was in need of a rethink in her choice of wardrobe, whilst volunteer number two could possibly benefit by wearing darker shades of browns and greens. I must admit to having found the experience fascinating and would, given sufficient time, have been curious to find out if my own choice of a dark blue pin-stripe suit, white shirt and red tie was 'doing it' for me – and the audience.

And then came the best part. When Nadine sat down after her ten minutes, virtually the entire audience of women presented their business cards to her and requested either further information or an appointment.

What Nadine achieved in just ten minutes is what this book is all about. Yes, she was going to produce leaflets, brochures and build a website, but there was nothing to beat the power of her presentation or the amazingly effective live demonstration of her service. Quite simply, Nadine's mini workshop inspired the audience and they wanted more.

Doubtless you can now think of other examples of Seminar Selling:

- The wine importer who offers wine appreciation lessons.
- The florist who gives flower arranging workshops in her shop.
- The hairdresser who demonstrates how to achieve different cuts and styles.
- The firm of accountants that run workshops on how to minimise tax.
- The financial adviser who holds retirement and pension planning seminars.
- The presentation skills coach who holds speech workshops for grooms, fathers of the bride and the best man.
- The vets who run workshops on pet care for children and their parents.
- The antique dealers who run workshops on how to value china, glass and furniture.
- The restaurant owner who offers cookery classes.
- The broker who runs mortgage workshops for first-time-buyers.

- The interior designers who demonstrate how to make your home more attractive prior to putting it up for sale.

And so on. Take a moment now to think of a creative way you could promote your own business at either a seminar or workshop. Write down three ideas to demonstrate your product or service that would be of real benefit to existing or potential customers:

1.

2.

3.

Another great example of Seminar Selling at its finest was when Black & Decker were looking for ways to make its excellent power tools more attractive to the professional builder and not just the DIY enthusiast.

Their new professional brand was DeWALT, a name synonymous with quality, strength, performance and power. But it was no good just telling potential customers how good the tools were – they needed people to *see and try them* for themselves. So the company embarked on a massive campaign of live outdoor demonstrations where builders could come from far and wide to see and try the tools. They could cut things in half, drill holes, nail things together and hammer and saw to their hearts' content. They even ran the Million Dollar Challenge – an incredible nationwide competition where builders, contractors and power tool enthusiasts compete in regional heats to win a million dollars.

All they had to do was sink five screws into a piece of wood in the shortest possible time. There were over 400 qualifying events across the United States and Canada to find just 14 finalists who would compete for one million dollars. The 2002 winner ('King of the Drill') was Jon Smith, a general contractor from Delaware, Ohio who drove five screws in a very respectable 6.77 seconds. Well done Jon!

At the time of writing, the 2003 heats are well under way, with this year over 500 special events being staged for over 100,000 competitors. Specially fitted Million Dollar Challenge vehicles are visiting power tool retailers, construction sites and home centres where, according to the DeWALT website, people 'can test their prowess driving screws with a cordless drill'.

Great fun. And if you missed the action, you can see video clips on the company website. I wonder which brand of power tools Jon and all the other contestants will be using for the rest of their lives?

So we can see that although there have been incredible advances in communication technology, it is the high-visibility, high-touch approach which really hits the spot.

BENEFITS OF SEMINAR SELLING TO THE BUSINESS OWNER

- Potential customers get to see and experience you, your product and your service in action, before they make a purchase.

- Just holding the event at all positions you as an expert on the subject concerned – if not *the* expert. And the simple act of standing and using visuals as part of a sales related activity can increase the amount prospects are prepared to spend by about 25%!

- Seminar Selling is incredibly cost effective. Even if you don't charge a fee for attendance, consider your current cost of acquiring a customer and compare it to the cost of having a room full of warm customers. The fact that they have turned up at all makes them warm by definition, so you have multiple prospects all present at the same time.
- Seminar Selling is even more cost effective if you charge an entry fee. In fact if you do, your delegates or attendees are paying to be your prospects! We will explore the pros and cons of charging an entry fee in Chapter 4.
- Hosting a seminar or workshop gives you the opportunity to promote additional products and services, thus making the event even more profitable. More on this in Chapter 7.
- Speaking to a room full of people and *just demonstrating your expertise* actually takes the pressure off you, as you are not overtly trying to sell your product or service. I repeat, seminars are a demonstration of your expertise and the chance for people to see what you do 'live', so there is no need to make a blatant sales pitch for business.
- Seminars enable people to form a more detailed and valued opinion about you. This helps them to build trust without having to speak to you. They can also look at the reactions of other people in the audience and gauge how they too are responding.
- Conversion rates at seminars can be extremely high. By conversion rates, I mean people who approach you later with a view to purchasing your main product or service, or who approach you for a personal consultation based on your expertise. Andrew Brown, a financial adviser based in the South

West of England wrote to me: *'(Our) seminars would typically be attended by between 35–55 people, and the conversion rate was always extremely high and often approaching 100%.'* Enough said.

- Of those attendees who do not subsequently approach you, you have at least warmed them up for another day. A key skill in Seminar Selling is relationship building, so that even if they are not ready to make a purchase now, they may wish to in future. We will show you how to do this within your presentation in Part 2.

- Holding a seminar or workshop can massively increase your list of contacts for your newsletter. Regular communication with customers or potential customers is essential for any small business and a newsletter is an ideal way of doing this. Ideally I would recommend an email newsletter and in Chapter 6 we'll show you how to use email newsletters to support your business, support your seminars, drive people to your website and increase sales.

- Some people find that after holding a few seminars or workshops, new doors unexpectedly start to open for them. It is possible to get very well known in a particular field and consequently be in demand as an expert speaker on your subject. Some people even find their seminars are so successful that their expertise becomes more in demand than their main product or service. This also can lead to more speaking work, private consultations and consequently the need to completely re-engineer their business.

BENEFITS OF SEMINAR SELLING TO ATTENDEES

- The most important benefit of seminars or workshops to attendees is that your event enables them to build up a picture for themselves of the quality of your product or service. Rather than rely on a third party's recommendation, they can judge for themselves if your service is right for them – either now or in the future. Your presentation is, for them, the living embodiment of your business and the perception they build will be all that matters.

- Any business that relies heavily on a service-based proposition needs to build a relationship with its customers. Equally, customers need to have a relationship with your business and seminars provide an excellent opportunity for people to get to know a business before moving to the next stage – be it a personal consultation or to make their purchase.
- People like to receive information in different ways. Many business owners wrongly make assumptions about how customers and prospects will want to receive information about their product or service – with written information being at the top of the list. Unless you know *exactly* how your customers like to receive information, offer it in a variety of formats. One of the most under used is the seminar format, where people can engage many more senses – thus increasing the likelihood of your message being remembered and acted upon.

  Motivational speaker Patricia Tucker provides a good example. Trish talks about how business people can increase their passion, energy and enthusiasm for their work and thus revitalise themselves and their business. As part of her excellent presentation, she gives everyone in the audience a taste of her Passion Potion – a deep pink, healthy juice drink with a secret ingredient! Quite apart from the quality and content of her message, by giving everyone a taste of the Passion Potion, she is engaging not only people's senses of sight and sound, but also touch, taste and smell – not to mention their imaginations!

- Don't make assumptions about *why* people attend seminars. Stimulating as your presentation may be, there are some people who come along just for the lunch or the 'freebies'. Yes, there are always a few like this in every audience and you'll find plenty at exhibitions and trade shows! If you do take a stand at these events, make sure that you have attractive carrier bags made up with your company name and website address, so that people have something in which to carry all their freebies. But make sure that *your* carrier bags are the LARGEST as you will find that people put all the other bags they collect inside the largest. Yours needs to be on the *outside*!

Networking

There are also many people who attend seminars or workshops purely for the networking opportunity. By networking, you are not only finding new business contacts but are, in effect, promoting yourself in the subtlest of ways – much like Seminar Selling.

Don't underestimate the importance of the networking aspect for attendees. It is a vital part of business life, so let people network to their hearts' content during the various breaks. In fact, *encourage it* by including it in your promotional material as one of the benefits of attending your seminar e.g. *superb networking opportunity!* In the United States (where it is estimated that there are approximately 20,000 seminars every day) they see the networking aspect as one of the key benefits of attending.

THE KEYS TO SUCCESS

So it can be seen that the benefits of promoting your products or services in a live environment are considerable. Personally, I think the keys to the success of Seminar Selling are threefold:

First, there is the aspect of clarity. Attendees are given an opportunity to see you and/or your product in action – warts and all – and this gives them the chance to get answers to the questions they want answered.

Second, by seeing you or your service in action, they are able to 'try before they buy', or put a toe in the water prior to committing themselves further.

Third, there is the social aspect. By sitting anonymously in an audience of people, attendees can observe other people's reactions to you, they can network for new business contacts and the social warmth of a gathering with likeminded people helps to oil the wheels of the sales cycle.

But despite the many benefits of this sales approach, many business people resist holding seminars. There are natural concerns about the amount of planning involved and lack of experience in marketing such events. Over the next two chapters we look at how to plan your seminars or workshops and how to market them to get 'bums on seats'.

> 'The Million Dollar Challenge accomplished two key strategic objectives for DeWALT.
>
> First, our distribution base looks to us to create events at their stores that generate excitement and provide reasons for their customers to make purchases. By creating a national event with a theme, we were able to stretch tight budgets by getting other manufacturers, such as Chevrolet, Carhartt Clothing, and others to join with us and financially support the events, thereby making the whole promotion

bigger than what we could have done on our own. Second, we increased brand affinity for DeWALT with our key construction end users, who were able to satisfy their desire to compete with skills that they use on their jobs every day. In the end, we awarded the million dollar prize at a NASCAR (National Association for Stock Car Auto Racing) event and our driver won the race that day, making it one of the most exciting days in DeWALT history.'

Nolan D. Archibald, Chairman and Chief Executive Officer
of The Black & Decker Corporation

4

Planning Your Seminars and Workshops

'Defining your target market is key.

Do your research – think about their lifestyle – where might they go, what else they buy and how they like to buy. Thinking laterally can open up some amazingly cost-effective promotional routes. Once you have your target customer defined, take a critical eye at your sales process, ensuring that at each stage you are meeting or preferably exceeding client expectations. This is nothing groundbreaking, but something that a number of businesses seem to overlook these days.

We take communication with our clients, written or verbal extremely seriously and a bugbear of mine is to be promised a call by Friday and not to receive it. Regardless of whether you have anything to tell your client, if you promised you would call, call!

From the first contact to the final invoice you have countless opportunities to get your brand and what it stands for in front of your client, so make the most of them.'

Jacqui Smith, Director, HomeSmiths Ltd

The planning of your event is, surprisingly, a relatively easy part of the process – provided that a few important rules are followed closely. A key objective of the planning process is to 'get bums on seats' and Chapter 5 will examine the best way to go about marketing and promoting your events.

In this chapter, we look at everything else you need to do to make sure your seminar or workshop is a success and I strongly suggest you follow my 'Rule of Five'.

5 months + 5 decisions + 5 planning stages
= successful seminar selling

WHEN DO I START PLANNING MY SEMINAR?

The most important piece of advice I can give in this book is not to underestimate the amount of time needed to plan and market your seminars. This is not because there is so much work to do, but more to give you enough time to make sure that what *must* be done, actually gets done. After all, until seminars become integrated into your day-to-day activities, you still have a business to run and there will probably be greater priorities with which to concern yourself.

Give yourself a full five months to set up your first seminars, after which you should be able to move to a three-month cycle as you learn from your first few events. So, if you want to hold your first seminar on, for example, 13 November, you need to start work on it on 13 June. But even in this example you may want to consider starting work earlier because key helpers are likely to be on holiday at some stage during the process.

WHAT ARE THE FIVE MAIN DECISIONS THAT NEED TO BE MADE?

Decision 1 – What are my objectives for the event?

Your seminars or workshops will fail unless you have a clear objective for what *you* want to achieve. As they say – if you fail to plan, you plan to fail. Make sure too that you have a separate objective for what you want *the delegates to do* as a result of attending your seminars. On the surface it sounds like these two objectives will be the same, however there is a subtle but important difference between what *you want to achieve* and what *you want the attendees to do* as a result of your presentation. The two objectives together will provide very clear focus for your events.

Here are some examples of objectives for *you*. Do you want to:

- Increase awareness of your company locally, nationally (or internationally)?
- Increase awareness of your product or service locally (or wider)?
- Increase sales locally, nationally (or internationally)?
- Increase your customer base?
- Enhance your reputation for quality goods and services?
- Enhance your reputation as being the leading experts in your field?
- Draw attention to other products and services that sell less well?
- Announce new products or services?
- Build relationships and strategic partnerships with other businesses?
- Offer a social event for loyal customers and their friends? (Remember 'and their friends' for later.)
- Pass on your expertise to others?
- Prove the worth or effectiveness of your product or service through demonstration?
- Try out a new distribution route?

These and others could be objectives for your events and only you will know what is appropriate for your business. But you *must* have objectives, as they will provide direction for everything you do in the planning and promotional phases. Next – write them down, keep them visible and refer back to them regularly, particularly on the day of the seminar.

Your objectives will also guide you on the type of event you wish to hold. Here are some suggestions:

- A whole day seminar or workshop.
- A half day (morning or afternoon) seminar or workshop.
- A breakfast meeting.
- A lunchtime event.
- An evening event.
- A weekend boot camp (either at home or abroad).
- An open day at your place of work with ongoing demonstrations.
- A networking or social event.
- Industry exhibitions, trade shows and fairs.
- Craft fairs and county shows.
- A showcase, talk or presentation at business clubs.

Try to choose the format that best suits your objectives, your subject matter and the type of person you are targeting.

Decision 2 – What should be the subject matter?

Your subject matter will be guided by your main objective and should focus on what it is that you want people to take away, remember and act upon. And when you think about it, this is crucial. Your attendees must act if you are to get the high conversion rates needed to increase profits. In a later chapter we look at some other ways to decide on content and specific presentation skills which will help people to remember much more of what you tell them and thus increase the likelihood of them being motivated to talk to you in person after the event.

Within the context of your objective, your subject matter should not be too broad or too wide-ranging, as this will lessen its overall appeal. Generally speaking, the more niche the subject matter, the higher the likely level of interest. That is not to say that a talk or presentation at a generic level won't have appeal, but what will have more appeal is if the generic level is narrowed.

For example, a demonstration on watercolour painting will certainly have appeal to many, but a demonstration on landscape watercolour painting will have greater appeal. Of greater appeal still will be a demonstration on autumn landscape watercolour painting.

Financial advisers, as another example, should take care to strike a balance between being too generic in their approach and not going so far as to talk about one particular product from one life office or investment company. One approach could be to show potential clients how they can minimise inheritance or capital gains tax through financial products.

The important thing in all seminars is not to cross over the line to the point where you appear to be selling a specific product. Successful Seminar Selling is about enhancing the perception of your expertise – not overtly selling. Feel free to demonstrate your product or service by all means, but make absolutely sure that people can see how they would benefit or how it would enhance their lives.

Decision 3 – Who are my target audience and how many should attend?

Again, the target audience will be guided by the objective of your event and having a clear target audience will make your promotion easier.

A key question is whether you want an audience full of existing customers or potential customers. The answer is of course both. Existing customers should be more predisposed to attending and, ultimately, are more profitable. New prospects offer the potential to grow your customer base, which in turn should increase further as they refer you to other people over time.

Different types of customers require a different marketing approach, which we will examine in the next chapter. Whatever your proposed mix of audience members, always consider the potential networking opportunities for them and wherever possible try to get at least a small number of your personal friends to be present. A few friendly faces in the crowd will put you at ease.

How many people should attend?

The more niche your event the fewer will attend, but the greater likelihood of them eventually becoming a customer. Your numbers will also be influenced by the budget you have and your venue. If you are putting on a demonstration in your shop or office premises, clearly it is easier to make a decision on numbers. If you think you have the potential to get 100 people along, then you will need to look at larger venues.

Decision 4 – Should I charge a fee for attendance?

Whilst it is not essential, charging a fee for attendance can make a huge difference in the level of your profits from seminars and has other advantages too. However, many seminar hosts resist charging an entry fee for fear that people will not pay to attend.

This could not be further from the truth and I have seen no evidence to show that a sensible, but worthwhile fee puts off people from attending. Indeed, charging a fee actually *increases their perception of the value of the event* and attendees will be paying to be your prospects! Furthermore, the more niche your market, the higher price you can charge.

How much should I charge?

If we use the example of a whole day workshop as a guide, you can adjust the price accordingly for shorter events. Anything from £75 to £250 appears typical for whole day events across a variety of industries and I personally have charged £147 per ticket, or £97 for early booking. As an alternative I have charged £127 per ticket for purchases of two or more, or £87 for the equivalent 'early-bird' price. Before we talk about discounts, let's do a quick sum.

Imagine you get 40 people to attend at the early-bird price of £97 and a further 20 at the full price of £147. That's £6,820 before you've even said a word and will cover the cost of the event many times over. Now imagine that (let's be generous) 25% of the attendees want to make an appointment with you and eventually purchase your main product or service – you can soon start to see how the profits increase dramatically. Not only is it possible to achieve conversion rates at this level and higher, but in Chapter 7 we'll show you how to multiply these profits many times over.

Discounts and incentives

I won't deny that charging a fee seems a very big step for many potential seminar and workshop hosts, but although the fee itself will enhance the perception of the event's quality and value it is possible to manipulate the entrance fee to make it more attractive.

In fact your discounted price should be your 'real' price, so set your advertised price at a high level but expect people to pay the lower amount, e.g. £97 as opposed to £147 in the example above. Also offer discounts for multiple bookings and discounts for members of various business groups, including Business Link, Institute of Directors, Federation of Small Businesses, local business clubs, Women in Business Clubs, Chamber of Commerce, Round Table, export clubs, trade associations, e-business clubs and networking and referral groups (e.g. Business Network International or BNI). In addition you can offer discounts for booking on-line and you can offer a discount if people quote a special reference number from an advertisement. (The latter also helps to track which promotional method is most effective.) Many people are still not entirely comfortable booking anything online, so why not offer a discount for booking by fax or even by text message?

Look out too for any subsidies that might be available which can help to bring down the price of your tickets. The European Social Fund (ESF) for example has objectives which, amongst other things, include improving and developing the skills of employed people, tackling long-term unemployment, improving training opportunities, encouraging entrepreneurship and promoting equal opportunities for women in the workplace. So in the case of your own seminars and workshops, if your events are deemed to qualify and assist in these aims, some of your attendees may be able to claim a refund of a substantial portion of the price of their ticket.

In my own experience, the combination of charging an entry fee and attendees being able to obtain a discount is an extremely powerful draw. On the one hand the entry fee enhances the perception of the value of the event, yet on the other attendees believe they are getting a real bargain if they don't have to pay full price.

Even if your event is not the sort where there is the potential for attendees to receive a subsidy, offer discounts anyway! As we will see in the next chapter much of the success of your events will depend on getting bums on seats. A really effective way of doing this is to offer a free ticket for every ticket paid for, or three for the price of two. Many people feel more comfortable if they attend seminars with a friend or colleague, so make it easy for them to bring someone along by offering them a free ticket with their own. Don't worry if that eats into your profits – you'll discover later how the free entrants will soon become profitable!

In short, be as flexible as you can on how people make a booking, how they pay for it and what they pay. If someone wants to book and they don't fall into any discountable categories, still find a reason to offer them a discount. When people call to ask if they qualify or to say that they have just missed the early booking discount, tell them you are in a good mood today or that the sun is shining or it's your cat's birthday – just make sure that everyone gets a discount. Don't forget, the way you deal with people at this stage tells them a lot about you and your business. Make sure that you come across as friendly, professional and flexible. Once they have bought you as a person, they will buy your product or service – guaranteed.

Other incentives

At the end of the day I believe that it is the content of your events which primarily drives the decision as to whether someone will attend or not, because subconsciously they are asking themselves 'What's in it for me?' But there are other things you can do to convince people to pay to attend.

1. Offer a full refund. Offering a full refund if the customer is not completely satisfied with their goods is often seen in shops and stores. There is no reason why you can't do the same if an attendee at your event is not completely satisfied. Offering a full refund is almost a challenge to find fault and also shows that you are extremely confident in the quality of your seminar or workshop.

2. Bonus materials. There's a lot of talk in business at the moment about the importance of providing 'added value' to customers. But whatever it is that you provide by way of added value, it must be tangible in the eyes of the recipient. It will have even more value to them if they think it is exclusive to them or to a business group of which they are a member. We will cover this further in Chapter 5 of this book, but wherever possible specify to potential attendees the 'extras' that they will receive for attending and try to quantify their value – thus giving the impression that *only* attendees at your event will receive them.

Decision 5 – Location, date and time

The location of your event will often be determined by the nature of your business. If you are a florist for example, your own shop premises would be ideal, but you would undoubtedly be restricted by space. In this situation, a good solution would be to run a regular series of quite short flower arranging demonstrations, each perhaps lasting about 45 minutes to an hour. Think about who your attendees will be and work out from there when they would be most likely to be able to attend. Of course there is nothing to stop you from using another venue.

Hotels are the most obvious choice, though unless you go very upmarket they often lack atmosphere and can be a bit pricey if you are not charging an entry fee. On the plus side, most are geared up for virtually any type of meeting event, have plenty of parking and usually have all the necessary presentation equipment to hand. In addition refreshments are easily available. In short, much of the hassle of putting on a seminar or workshop will be taken care of by someone else – but that's what you are paying for. My concern about using hotels is not so much the cost, but that many of the chains are a bit 'samey' and sanitised. Again, unless you have chosen a fabulous five-star hotel, there will be no curiosity value for attendees, so try to find slightly unusual venues where the setting itself has the potential to offer added value.

I recently assisted at a seminar in Knightsbridge in the heart of London. The venue for the event was a private ladies club, which made for extremely elegant surroundings and meticulous attention to detail.

I have also used Denbies Wine Estate in Dorking, Surrey as a seminar venue. Dorking is an old market town some 25 miles south of the centre of London and boasts England's largest vineyard and a magnificent chateau-style visitor centre. When building the centre they were clearly aware of their potential as a conference venue and include as part of their delegate rate:

- A high quality buffet lunch (their food is Egon Ronay recommended).
- A Wine Experience tour of the working winery on a specially made people mover.
- A special effect 360° film.
- A tasting of their magnificent wines in the atmospheric cellars.

Denbies also has a superb shop where, naturally, the visitor or seminar attendee will not be able to resist making a purchase from a huge range of high quality goods and wines. As a location for a workshop or seminar, Denbies Wine Estate has much to offer and is likely to be far more attractive as a venue for your attendees than yet another hotel conference room.

And of course, Denbies is in itself a fine example of a business that benefits from Seminar Selling in more ways than one. After a whole day event I ran at the venue, my delegates went off for their film, tour and tasting and over an hour later they each emerged from the shop clutching several bottles of the local produce. Not only did they enjoy a fine workshop on the benefits of Seminar Selling, but they also proved the concept worked by patronising the venue itself.

If you have trouble finding a venue for your events, you can always employ the services of a venue finding service. The British Association of Conference Destinations (*www.bacd.org.uk*) or The Conference People (*www.confpeople.co.uk*) are good places to start. Both offer a free venue finding service. But wherever you choose, make absolutely sure that it is easy to get to and easy to find!

Do your research:

- Can you set up the night before?
- Is access to your venue hindered by rush hour traffic?
- Is the venue within five minutes of a motorway junction?
- Is the venue within a short drive (or walk) from a railway or underground station?
- Will the venue allow you to pay on the day or after your event?
- Does the venue provide maps?
- Does the venue have an attractive website (which includes directions)?
- Is the room you are using easy to locate at the venue immediately on arrival?
- If you are using several rooms for your seminar (e.g. for breakout sessions etc), are they all on the same floor of the venue or will people have to move between floors? (This can be a nightmare if your timings are tight.)
- Is there plenty of free parking?
- If a hotel, can you negotiate a discount for people who want to stay overnight?
- Are there any other local attractions, which could add value to your event?
- Can you negotiate a discount with local attractions, which could form part of your marketing?
- Can you get hold of testimonials from previous customers?

When people arrive at your event you want them to be in a positive, receptive and friendly frame of mind. If they have had to struggle through traffic it will be your fault – not theirs, even if they did get up late.

When is the best time and day to hold seminars?

Again, your type of business, objectives and your target audience will often dictate this. If, for example, your event is targeted at housewives or househusbands, then clearly the hours of 8am – 9am and between 3pm and 4.30pm are not advisable. Put yourself in their shoes and think carefully about when they are most likely to be able to attend or would want to attend.

If your target audience works during the day think about when the best time would be for them. Could you run a breakfast meeting, or a workshop at lunchtime? Provided your event has clear and specific benefits for carefully targeted groups of people, they will generally attend whatever the time of day. Having said that, some days are better than others.

Try to avoid Mondays and Fridays and in order of preference, aim for Thursdays, Wednesdays and then Tuesdays. There is a feeling in many businesses that the serious work is done in the first half of the week (particularly Mondays), but on Fridays many people are no longer in 'work mode'. Despite that, Fridays can be a good day if you are running a *whole day* event and people feel that they can better justify a full day out of the office. This is particularly the case if there is a good local attraction near your event venue which they could also visit. At the time of writing, I am planning a seminar at a hotel in Manchester, UK. The seminar is a whole day event and on a Friday. It will be finished by 4pm and the hotel is right next to Manchester United's Old Trafford stadium. As I said earlier, curiosity value is important.

When running whole day events, start them after the rush hour, wherever you are located. Even the most enthusiastic attendee won't want to be at your event for a full 9 to 5 day. Let them have a bit of a lie-in and go for 9.30am arrival and coffee, with a 10am start. That way everyone has a sporting chance of turning up. Be finished by 4pm to 4.30pm so that people can either go to a local attraction or get out before the rush hour moves into full swing. If you are targeting business people, avoid having an event that starts much later than 10.30am as many people will go to their office or place of work first. If they get stuck into something while they are there, then there is a good chance they will stay and will miss your seminar.

But there can also be regional differences if you are thinking of putting on an event away from your usual territory. For example, timing that works well for business people in Glasgow, Scotland does not necessarily work for people 70 kilometres along the M8 in Edinburgh.

What about evening events?

Avoid a Friday evening unless your event has a strong social element. Good days for evening seminars are Mondays and Tuesdays. Try to make sure that evening events are held within a short walking distance of a pub or wine bar and are finished by 10pm (10.30pm latest), as there is a good chance that many of your delegates will join you for a drink if you ask them. I'll explain why this happens later. Finally, the best days to run a boot camp or residential workshop are Saturdays and Sundays and we will look at these events in more detail later.

A few further thoughts on choosing dates.

- If you are targeting business people within specific trades or professions, remember to check to see if your proposed dates clash with industry events, exams or the run up to them. Not surprisingly, people taking exams will be less inclined to attend your events during this period.

- Avoid holding your events in any week which includes a public holiday. Many people take off the whole week as it reduces the amount of annual leave they need to use. I would also try to avoid the week immediately preceding one which includes a public holiday.
- Unless your product or service has specific benefits for people in the middle of summer (for example, if you manufacture ice cream), avoid holding an event between the middle of June and the beginning of September.
- Do hold your events at times that benefit from seasonal activity. Financial advisers, for example, would be advised to put on seminars prior to the end of the tax year.

Let's pause for a moment to recap before we move on.

- Give yourself five months or more to plan your first few seminars.
- Make five decisions:
  - What are my objectives for the event? You need objectives:
    - for you and/or your business
    - for your attendees to do as a result of your seminar.
  - What should be the subject matter?
  - Who are my target audience and how many should attend?
  - Should I charge a fee for attendance?
  - Location, date and time.

WHAT ARE THE FIVE PLANNING STAGES?

In its broadest form, all we really need to do is:

- Decide what we are going to talk about and to whom.
- Decide where we are going to put on our event and when.
- Promote the event.
- Turn up and talk.

And this is fine, but we need a little more detail.

The five planning stages are as follows. Keep to these and you won't go wrong. A handy Five Month Countdown can be found in the back of the book which shows exactly when during the five month period you should deal with each item.

1. Initial preparation

We will assume that we have already made our five decisions discussed earlier. In the initial preparation phase we concern ourselves with the early stages of promotion together with things that should not be left to the last minute (but which usually are and end up being more of a hassle than they might otherwise have been!).

Include in this phase:

- Based on your objectives for your event, work out the cost of it and allocate a budget. Whatever the nature of your business and the type of event you are planning, you will soon see why charging for entry is such a good idea. Even if you decide not to charge for entry, you will discover later in this book how you can still turn your seminar or workshop into a highly profitable enterprise.

- Write a marketing plan. Once this has been done, it will form the basis of a plan for future events. Naturally as you run more events, it will be updated and improved as you learn from mistakes made earlier. The next chapter will show what should be included in your plan.

- Decide if you want to have a promotional stand at your event. If you do not want to run to the expense of this, as an alternative talk to companies that make exhibition stands about pull-up or roller banners. These start from about £130 and can add a very professional look to your seminar – whatever business you are in. What's more, they are really easy to store, transport and set up.

- Put together a Gantt chart to show what needs to be done and by when.

- If you are seeking to develop strategic partnerships with other businesses, decide if you will have other speakers present and involve them in the planning.

- Make enquiries with local business groups, colleges or universities about grants or subsidies, which may be available to reduce the cost of your tickets.

- Start to build a relationship with the event or conference manager at your chosen venue (if it is not your own premises). For example, decide on timings for start, finish, coffee and tea breaks and agree lunch menus if appropriate. If you can build a relationship with the venue staff over your five-month period, believe me it will make a big difference on the day, particularly if there are any last minute hitches.

- Write a press release and send it to your local newspapers, television and radio stations. Invite the press to attend your event and offer to write an article on your area of expertise for the paper. In other words, start getting your name in the media, so that when your promotion starts properly, people will recognise your name.
- Decide if you want to record or film your event and contact production companies.
- Start to think about whether you will sell any 'back of room' products at your event. More on this in Chapter 7.
- Decide on a rough agenda for your seminar.
- Decide what equipment you will need on the day – e.g. flipcharts, pens, screen, projector, laptop computer, overhead projector etc.
- Start to spruce up your presentation skills. There is help later in this book and there are plenty of other books and courses available. (Visit www.trainingstrategies.co.uk for a list of good books.)

2. Promotion

The promotion of your event is the most important aspect of all the planning. The next chapter looks at this phase in detail, but for now I will mention three important aspects which will be repeated several times.

- Make sure that all your promotion is highly targeted. That's not to say that 'throwing enough mud in the hope that some will stick' is not a valid strategy, it's just that it takes a lot longer to get your message across to the people you want to hit. It's also the most expensive option.

- Secondly, although your promotion should be highly targeted, consider all possible methods of communication. Don't make assumptions about how people in your target market like to receive information.

- Because you won't be making assumptions about how people like to receive information, you will inevitably need to make changes to your normal marketing mix. Some changes need only be small, but they will be changes which will produce new income streams in their own right.

3. Final preparation

The final preparation stage predominantly covers confirmations and rehearsals. Included in this phase:

- Confirming advertising.
- Arranging any printing that is needed.
- Confirming any special equipment that needs to be hired.
- Finalising your PowerPoint presentation.
- Rehearsing your presentation (several times).
- Preparing feedback and evaluation forms.
- Acknowledging bookings.
- Preparing handouts.
- Booking your accommodation for the night before.
- Deciding what to wear on the day.
- Deciding how you will follow up attendees after the event.
- Arranging helpers and making sure they understand their roles.

4. Performance

The necessary presentation skills that you will need are covered in detail later on, but there is also much else that you should consider on the day of your seminar, including:

- Avoid a heavy full English breakfast, tea or coffee. Have something light that includes fruit. Drink fruit juice or water.
- Get access to the seminar room as early as possible. It always takes longer to set up than you imagine and allow time for last minute problems.
- Check your technology is working (even if you checked it the night before).
- Make sure you are completely set up before anyone arrives. You must be completely relaxed and unrushed to help ease any nerves. Once set up, try to get 20 to 30 minutes quiet time to yourself to look over your notes.
- If you do not have any secretarial support, make sure that your office phone is redirected to your mobile so that any non-attendees can get a message to you. Ideally you will want to speak to them in person. Alternatively, leave a message on your office answer phone to call you on your mobile. Some people cancel by email and so you may not see their message until after the event. Set up your email to include an 'out of office' note to call you.
- Continue to drink water (not too cold) and prepare your voice by reading out loud.
- Enjoy yourself!

5. Post performance

What you do after the event is just as important as what you do before and so you should carefully plan the post seminar activities. These should include:

- Sending out pre-prepared thank-you letters to attendees – but including your *handwritten* comments which reflect anything interesting that happened or was said on the day. Also include answers to any questions that you could not deal with at the seminar and make reference to individual comments made by people during the seminar.
- Contacting anyone who you were expecting but who did not attend.
- Analysing the feedback sheets and taking note for future events.
- Sending out a press release describing how the event benefited local attendees. If the press did not attend the event (there's never any guarantee that they will), have someone take a photo during your talk and include it with your release. Make sure you continue to build a relationship with the press, both locally and in the specialist press for your industry. Build on your image as an expert and this will feed through into future events which you hold. The more you contribute to the press, the more you will be perceived as an expert on your subject and the more people will want to attend your seminars. The more people that attend your seminars, the more people will purchase your main product or service. They will also purchase other products that you have which support your seminars and we will look at this in detail in Chapter 7.
- Put in place a structured plan to contact attendees at regular intervals over the weeks and months after the event. This may include inviting them to another event in future (also see boot camps).

SUMMARY

You can of course do too much planning for your seminars or workshops and you run the risk of getting completely bogged down in the minutiae of it all. But I do recommend that for at least your first two or three events you try to follow some sort of plan, even if it is conceived in a pub or on the back of a cheque book. Providing you have clear objectives for what you are trying to achieve, you will find the planning stage both enjoyable and fulfilling. You will learn a great deal along the way and before long you will work out your own way of planning and promoting your events.

But our Rule of Five is a great way to start:

5 months + 5 decisions + 5 planning stages = successful seminar selling

5

The Golden Rules of Marketing Your Seminars

Understanding your business and ensuring that you are visible is crucial to success. Tony Raynor, Managing Director of Abbey Telecom, has been credited with some of the most innovative forms of marketing, including his 'whoisthis' campaign which used advertising on the side of newborn lambs.

> 'As a small business we cannot afford to spend huge amounts on marketing campaigns so we have to use innovative ideas that drive people to our website or make them pick up the phone.
>
> I met a farmer at a Round Table dinner and within the hour (and after a few glasses of wine) we agreed a sponsorship deal to provide raincoats for his newborn lambs. I knew that the bright orange raincoats would draw a lot of attention from passing motorists including several TV stations.'

The campaign objective was to drive visitors to a website and included integrating the 'lamb coats' with advertising on his own engineering vehicles and works uniforms.

> 'I had originally thought about just using Abbey Telecom and our logo but I realised that some people would be put off with a business advert so we developed the *www.whoisthis.co.uk* website. The site was an information resource for business marketers and it greatly increased our click through to the Abbey website. This in turn led to an increase in sales and all for a budget of under £1,000.

> By following the campaign through we benefited from a great deal of PR in both regional and national press, increased traffic on our website and finally, and most importantly, more sales for Abbey Telecom.'
>
> Tony Raynor

In modern Seminar Selling it is not sufficient just to have a room full of people to whom you make a nice presentation, in the hope that some will come up to you later with a view to purchasing your products or service. Don't get me wrong – this is a good start, but there is very much more to making your event a seriously profitable enterprise. Much more.

The marketing of your seminar or workshop is not just to promote your event, but is integral to the presentation of you, your business, your service and your expertise. In fact your seminar starts the moment you start marketing the event. As I hinted at earlier in the book, to promote your events you will undoubtedly have to make changes to your current marketing mix and it is the nature of these changes that will make the difference between just another seminar and a seminar which changes your fortunes forever. In the next chapter we will help you to make changes which will not only promote your event, but which will produce profitable new income streams in their own right.

But let's start with a few golden rules.

The most important point to remember is that your seminars are not a showcase for your main product or service. They are a showcase for **your expertise** and it is the attendees' perception of your expertise which will lead to sales of your product or service. Unless you have a substantial and specific budget to promote and run your seminar, it must at least break even and should preferably be income generating in its own right. So to ensure that they do break even, or, to make your events as profitable as possible you need to find attendees in the most cost effective ways possible. If you follow the rules below, you will not only promote the events, but will be well on your way to creating an exciting new income stream.

1. DISCOVER WHAT WORKS BEST FOR YOU

Whatever marketing methods you adopt, measure the results. It is absolutely vital to make careful notes of what *you* find to be most effective in a) getting people to attend and b) getting people to make additional purchases from you. A marketing method that works well for me may not necessarily be the best for you and just because one person finds text messaging effective in promoting their seminar does not mean someone else will. We are all in different businesses in different parts of the country with different clients; so when a promotional method works for you, make a detailed note of what you did and why. But. . .

2. DON'T RULE OUT ANY PARTICULAR METHOD OF PROMOTION

Make sure that you try a full range of both online and traditional offline promotional methods first and do not make assumptions about how you think people want to receive information. Communication technology is developing fast and so provides people with several different ways of sending and receiving information.

Equally, don't make assumptions about how people want to make contact with you. Provide a full range of ways for people to register for your seminar, including:

- email
- via your website
- telephone (with a freephone number)
- 24-hour telephone answering machine
- fax
- text message
- post (letter, postcards etc with either postage paid or a freepost address)
- face-to-face.

3. MAKE YOUR EVENT IRRESISTIBLE!

In all your promotional activity you must strive to make your event difficult to ignore by your target audience. Do this by constantly stressing the **benefits** of attending your event. Benefits, benefits, benefits and then some more benefits! Without the big marketing budgets of large corporations, small businesses have to make every communication count. And one of the best ways of doing this is to focus strongly on how, specifically, your seminar or workshop will help or improve the lives of attendees.

4. OFFER BONUSES FOR ATTENDANCE

After you have stressed the benefits, offer bonus materials for attending your event. For people who have made a decision to attend based on the advertised content, bonus materials are like the icing on the cake and help to reassure them that they have made the right decision. For other people, what appear to be free, but high value bonuses will help to make the event irresistible so that they come to the right decision.

Bonuses do two more things. Firstly people feel that they are getting more than they are paying for. Something for free when they make a purchase has always been an effective draw and works particularly well in the seminar market. Secondly, as we'll discover shortly, your seminars must offer very high content for attendees and by offering bonus materials for attendance, people subconsciously believe that they will not be short-changed on content at the seminar itself.

What bonuses should I offer?

First of all, your bonuses for attendance should genuinely be of high value. People must believe that you really are giving them something that is not only valuable to them but to you too – like your time. Here are some examples:

- Half an hour free consultation with you – valid for 12 months after the event.
- Free question and answer email advice for 12 months after the event.
- 25% discount on any purchase of your main product or service.
- A free sample of your main product.
- A free e-book showing attendees how to. . .
- A free CD recording of your event, which is only available to attendees.
- A weekly email after your event containing extra tips and advice.
- Discounts for early and/or multiple bookings.
- Discounts for members of a variety of business clubs and groups.
- 50% discount on future seminars or events that you hold.
- A full refund if not completely satisfied.

Ideally, you should state the actual value of the bonuses to help convince people that they really are worth something in cash terms. For example, in the case of the half-hour consultation, you should say 'Worth £100' or whatever your actual fee is.

5. GET HELP!

The secret behind really good promotion of a seminar is to get other people to do it for you, or to be precise – with you. Not only that, you want your promotion to be as effective as possible and for the lowest possible cost. Why make life harder for yourself when you can spread the load by asking friends and business associates to help?

Who could help?

i) Business groups, clubs and associations

If you are the owner of a small business there is a good chance that you are a member of a national or local business club or association. It could be the local Rotary, Chamber of Commerce, Business Link, export club, networking group etc and this means you have access to dozens, if not hundreds or thousands of other business people, many of whom may want your product or service. These clubs and associations are always looking for new members, so offer them a free advertisement in your seminar handout, leaflet or workbook. If the latter, be generous and offer a free full page in exchange for them mentioning your event at one (or more) of their regular club meetings. They may also be prepared to include your event in their club magazine or paper.

You may even be able to get the club to sponsor your event. They will want their logo on your promotional materials and website, but this will add extra credibility to your seminar.

Quite apart from the fact that your event will be promoted free of charge to local business people, you can also consider approaching club members direct and offering them an incentive for every booking they are able to obtain. This works particularly well if you are charging a fee for attendance and you can offer people a commission for each ticket they sell on your behalf. But make the commission extremely worthwhile. Go to as much as 50% of the face value of the ticket if your costings can take it. Let's say you are selling tickets at £77 each and someone sells ten for you, that would put nearly £400 straight into their pocket and you have a further ten attendees that you would probably never have found. And there's always a good chance that each of those ten people will tell another ten people about your seminar and who could also become customers of yours. This is quite apart from any 'back of room' products they might purchase at the seminar itself.

ii) Newspapers and magazines

Just like business groups above, there is great potential to obtain free publicity from newspapers and magazines.

A journalist friend once told me to create news out of everything your business does and to tell your local and industry press accordingly. Do the same with your seminar – however small your business is. If it's newsworthy it will be printed.

Send a press release to your local newspaper about your seminar or workshop, explaining what your event is about and how people will benefit. Read the news articles on the first two or three pages of your local paper to get a feel for their style. Then try to write your release in the same way so that a busy editor need only directly copy what you have written. Remember to send a professionally taken photograph and include a quote from yourself, which can also be copied directly, e.g.:

> 'Proprietor, Susan Collins commented today: 'We're really excited about the open day in November. We've had so many customers ask us over the years about our recipes and how we make our jams, so this will be a superb opportunity for people to see the process in action. What's more, there will be free samples to take away.'

Always follow up your press release with a telephone call. Don't hassle the editor or ask them if they are going to print something, but enquire politely if they received the release and whether they have all the information they need. You can also offer to write an article about your area of expertise and explain how this would benefit both the paper and its readers. Remember – benefits, benefits, benefits.

Finally, some local papers will be very happy to 'sponsor' your event by putting their name to it. Offer to present your seminar 'in association with the *County Times*' for example, in exchange for them giving you a free advertisement or for publishing an article about your business. Explain that you are happy to publicise the paper in all your promotional materials and seminar handouts without charge if they are able to help you in this way. Although the newspaper will have little, if any involvement in the event, the lending of their name will enhance the credibility of your seminar.

Equally, if there is a specialist magazine serving your industry you can try the same approach, only do it earlier as magazine content is decided much further in advance. The newspaper or magazine concerned may even be prepared to give you free copies to give out to your attendees, again enhancing the value of the event.

iii) Radio stations

Whilst the UK is not particularly well served for a choice of good speech-based radio stations, BBC local radio offers an excellent service. There are many commercial stations too, but these generally have far less speech-based material. Either way, make the effort to build a relationship with your local stations. Local commercial radio works hard at not just entertaining, but at adding value and is often open to suggestions for new slots as long as it fits in with their format. You may be able to suggest a new slot which will not only hold you up as the local expert, but which should also get you a great deal of free publicity. Even if you can't get a regular slot, if you have taken the trouble to build a relationship and are seen as friendly and personable, there is a good chance that you could be featured on a 'phone in' or even interviewed. Remember – make news out of your events.

iv) Friends, staff and colleagues

In much the same way as in i) above, offer real incentives for friends and colleagues to promote your seminar. The number of people you can potentially reach is multiplied many times over if you have several people helping you. But as mentioned earlier, you must make it worth their while.

v) People in similar businesses

Don't shy away from approaching people in a similar business to yourself. Remember, the object of the exercise is to get bums on seats and ideally, **targeted** bums on seats. Where better than the customers of similar businesses? Approach these businesses directly and offer a 50% share of any registrations obtained as a result of contacting their list of customers.

Businesses share lists of customers all the time. Not all will let you contact their customers, but given sufficient incentive they will! And if anything, your event could help to resurrect a customer who has been long forgotten. Benefits all round – everyone wins.

vi) Bring a friend

A great way to dramatically increase attendance is to tell people that they can bring a friend or colleague. Very often this approach can double the number of your attendees. And if you are charging for attendance you can either offer the friend's ticket at half price, or even free. It works – try it!

By now you should be able to see a number of cost effective ways to get a room full of attendees for your event, whether a small gathering in your shop or office premises or something a little larger in a hotel or other venue. In the next chapter, we look at various aspects of the promotion in more detail.

6

Offline and Online Marketing and Promotion

'Businesses don't want radio commercials, they want advertising that works. The biggest mistake radio advertisers make is that they think creativity will generate a higher response rate. This is not true. Creativity 'in itself' won't persuade anyone to buy a product or service. It is there to lead the listener's mind in the direction we want it to go.

This sounds contradictory, but no matter how bizarre the scenario in your radio ad – always keep it real. If the listener can't connect with the scenario, they will not know what to do and why they should do it.'

Alan Bell, Chief Executive, Airforce

In the previous chapter we started to examine some of the rules of marketing your seminars. To recap, the really important points to remember are:

- Initially, unless you know your target market extremely well, do not rule out any particular type of promotional method.
- Do not make assumptions about how people want to receive information.
- Do not make assumptions about how people will want to register for your seminar. Provide a full range of options.

- Make your event irresistible to your target market, so they just *have* to attend.
- Provide a number of incentives to attend, such as discounts for early booking, discounts for bulk booking, discounts for members of business clubs and groups.
- Offer worthwhile bonuses for attendance and state their value.
- Encourage people who want to attend to bring a friend – either free or at a substantial discount.
- Work with business clubs, friends, colleagues, associates and other businesses to promote your events. Offer strong monetary incentives for each person they introduce and who registers to attend.
- Work with the local press to raise your company's profile by writing articles for their publication. Also, build relationships with local radio stations.
- Provide publicity for local business groups and media by offering them free advertising on your seminar promotional materials and handouts.
- Measure the effectiveness of everything you do. Take careful note of what works and what doesn't for next time.
- Whatever you do, constantly stress the benefits of your event. Remember – benefits, benefits and more benefits!

In short, work with as many people as possible to get your message out there. This is key to successful promotion of your event. It can be extremely hard work to do it all on your own and unless you have a large advertising budget you need as many people as possible helping you.

Essentially you have two main ways of promoting your events:

1. Offline promotion
2. Online promotion

1. OFFLINE PROMOTION

Until the arrival of the internet (which we have already discovered is wildly underused in the UK for e-commerce purposes), promotion was restricted to traditional offline activities. Predominantly these were, and still are:

- advertising in newspapers and magazines (both local and national)
- direct mail
- leaflet drops
- posters
- postcards
- telephone
- television and radio advertising
- audio and video
- business introducers
- public relations (PR)
- general correspondence.

A new addition to offline promotion is now bulk text or SMS (Short Message Service) messaging and we will look at this shortly. Meanwhile let's have a look at some of these promotional methods in more detail.

TELEVISION AND RADIO ADVERTISING

Television advertising is likely to be well out of reach of most small businesses until digital television becomes much more commonplace, but it is worth talking about the benefits of radio advertising in more detail.

Radio advertising for the promotion of your seminar can be extremely effective at a local level. It's not as expensive as you might think and there are a variety of packages available. Consider the facts.

According to research undertaken by the Radio Advertising Bureau, around two-thirds of the adult population tune in to radio each week and over 80% each month. There is a fairly even split in listening by gender, with 67% of men and 65% of women listening each week.

The favourite places for listening are generally those where radio accompanies another activity – e.g. in the car, over breakfast, in the bathroom and at the workplace. Radio often accompanies other media such as reading newspapers and magazines, surfing the internet and even watching television!

Around 65% of all adults listen to the radio in-car every week. Approximately 73% of in-car listeners fall into the ABC1 socio-economic group with 56% falling in to the C2DE group. The highest percentage of in-car listeners fall into the 25 to 44 age group, falling slightly for those aged 45 and above. The in-car audience has a strong skew towards upmarket, young to middle age men – an important audience who tend to be lighter commercial television viewers.

The good news is that over two-thirds of business people listen to commercial radio, and on average they will listen for over 12 hours a week – longer than they spend watching television. This is much higher than is usually assumed – in fact business people spend more time each day listening to radio than with any other key media (such as television, newspapers and magazines).

The importance of radio

Reflecting perhaps today's more relaxed working environment in modern Britain, radio listening at work has increased noticeably in recent years.

For advertisers who are targeting a business audience, the key issue is effective 'cut-through'. Conventional business media are very cluttered and business people have learned to edit ruthlessly – especially with printed media. And despite the fact that radio stations broadcast to millions of people, they are still talking to one person at a time. This is particularly significant to the businessperson alone in their car, because approximately 70% of listeners do not change channels when the advertisements are on. This differs from television viewers, where a similar percentage admit to flicking through the other channels when the advertisements start.

There is evidence to show that people feel a sense of trust in their radio station – very valuable in an age where television and newspapers are not as trusted as they used to be and there is good evidence to suggest that people actively listen to the radio even though they may be doing something else.

One of the most important points about radio though is that it is becoming more widely available: 8% of adults and 17% of 16 to 24 year olds already listen to the radio via the internet, 14% and 18% respectively listen to the radio via their television and 3% and 9% respectively listen to their radio via their mobile phone. Radio via a mobile phone is still relatively new technology, but when asked if they would listen via their phone if their handset had the facility, 20% of adults said they would.

In conclusion, despite the inexorable rise of the internet, radio is extremely important in the lives of its listeners and, combined with other media (which is often consumed simultaneously), radio can be extraordinarily effective. Quite apart from using the medium to promote your main business, it should definitely be considered as a way of promoting your seminars.

TELEPHONE

The telephone should certainly be considered as your preferred choice of marketing for existing clients. A relationship already exists for starters. Expect around half to say they are interested in your seminar and half of these to actually turn up.

For prospective clients, expect just over 1% of the people you talk to to say they are interested, and around 10% of these will actually turn up.

DIRECT MAIL

There are two types of direct mailshot: addressed mail and unaddressed mail.

Addressed mail

As I was putting out the dustbin for collection this morning, our postman Jim was just arriving. He reached inside his bag and said 'Shall I put these in the bin now and save you the trouble of taking them in the house?'

Not surprisingly, Jim's perception of the effectiveness of direct mail is a little prejudiced, but nevertheless it does have significant benefits.

Perhaps the main benefit of addressed direct mail is the ability to precisely target specific types of customer or potential customer. Combined with an infinite range of creative possibilities direct mail has much more going for it than you might imagine, though it's tempting to think that in our electronic age mail would be losing its appeal. But, when combined with a variety of other media it continues to offer enormous possibilities. And with modern data gathering techniques and the availability of third party databases, the accuracy of targeting and the effectiveness of targeted campaigns has been much improved.

The effectiveness of your campaign can be improved further if you think carefully about the delivery of your mailing. Always keep in mind who your target market is and adapt your message and language accordingly. Some things you might want to consider:

- **Have a powerful headline or title to your letter.** It should ideally be in the form of a question, implying that you have the answer – and that the answer will be of benefit to the reader if they take action. A strong title is vital, so make it count. Remember, benefits, benefits and more benefits. For example:

Looking for easy ways to increase the value of your home?

Have you ever wondered how to value antiques like the experts?

- **'Consider putting your headline or title in quotation marks.'** This gives the impression that someone actually said it so there is a human touch behind it.
- **Should the mailing be sent by first or second-class post?** First class is better, because the recipient of a second-class letter subconsciously feels it (and they) are not considered very important.
- **Would a handwritten envelope make a difference?** Again, put yourself in the shoes of the recipient. If it's handwritten it might be from a relative or friend and is far more likely to be opened.
- **What typeface should be used?** Wherever possible use a font which is easy to read, like Times New Roman or other 'serif' fonts like Palatino or Bookman Old Style.
- **Would the quality of the envelope and paper make a difference?** This depends on your market, but my view is always go for the best possible quality within the context of your target audience.
- **What is the best day for people to receive your mailing?** I am not convinced that it makes much difference what day of the week your mailing arrives, though there are schools of thought that suggest you should avoid mail arriving on a Monday. It's true that Monday's mail often seems to have less important stuff in it, so perhaps you don't want to give the impression that yours is not important too.
- Arrange the material in the envelope so that when opened, **the first thing people see is their name**. Using the recipient's name

makes the piece look more personal and should increase the chances of it being read.

- Always include a 'PS' at the end of your letter and make sure it includes one of the most important benefits of attending your seminar. The 'PS' is virtually always read, so it must contain a key benefit of attending.

Whatever you do with your mailings, always put yourself in the shoes of the recipient and do whatever it takes to get the piece opened and read. But the key factors are always going to be personal, precise targeting of your offering with information on specifically how your seminar will be of benefit.

Unaddressed mail

Although the ability to target customers using addressed mail is much more effective, unaddressed mail is growing in popularity. And don't we know it! Everything from brochures, leaflets, magazines, free samples and money-off vouchers are delivered to houses and businesses across the country every day.

But despite the apparent overload of direct mail, it can be extremely effective. Once it has dropped through your letterbox you do have to do something with it and for a brief moment you are forced to look at it. And if it's been carefully targeted there's a good chance you'll hold on to it for a little bit longer. In fact some types of unaddressed direct mail are deliberately retained – particularly catalogues and items that contain helpful information. I'm a firm believer that mailings of any description need to be particularly carefully targeted to be effective, but when promoting your seminars there can definitely be a place for unaddressed mail.

A supply of well-produced leaflets can be sent to a variety of different clubs and business groups for distribution to members and you can also arrange for leaflets to be inserted into copies of the local newspapers or magazines. Friends and colleagues too can distribute your leaflets and also consider including one with every piece of mail that leaves your office or business premises. In addition you can also do a local leaflet drop where you put one through the letterbox of every house or business in a certain area. Obviously, the more targeted you can make your leaflet drop, the better.

PRESS ADVERTISING

Paid press advertising

Traditional press advertising is, not surprisingly, the first port of call for many seminar hosts. You have the advantage of knowing that your advertisement is going to be seen by thousands, if not hundreds of thousands of people either in your local vicinity or wider still.

The general rule of thumb is that the more you advertise, the more your information will be seen and theoretically the greater likelihood of a response. It follows that the greater you want the response to be, the more you will have to pay. But it doesn't always have to be that way. Certainly creativity has a part to play in the effectiveness of your advertisement, as does clarity, perception of expertise, perception of value, targeting and the degree to which the benefits of attending are explained.

It is also extremely important to have some sort of properly organised advertising plan or campaign, rather than rely on just one big advertisement a week or two before your event. Business people who successfully use seminars as part of their overall marketing strategy will usually have developed their own advertising plans which they have put together through trial and error over time.

Positioning and frequency of your advertisements is also extremely important. Here's what independent financial adviser and regular seminar host, Andrew Brown says:

> 'We have always adopted a very direct approach [to advertising our seminars] and we found that to maximise the response to the event you would need a run of advertisements in the local press (in a prominent place in the paper – an 'early right' being ideal) over a four week period. A single advert would never be sufficient and the responses would tend to be greatest for the second week, with a considerable overflow into the third and final week prior to the event.
>
> The last advertisement should be at least a week beforehand and it was always beneficial to top up the numbers with invitations to both existing and potential professional introducers and a number of carefully selected clients.'

Free press advertising

There is nothing like getting free advertising when it comes to promoting your seminars! Advertising can take up a sizeable chunk of your budget, so anything you can get for free will help.

As we mentioned earlier, send regular press releases to your local paper and offer to write a series of articles. The editors will often pick up on a good press release and write an editorial. Sometimes it will just be a few lines and on other occasions something more substantial. Later on we will look at how to find material for your release.

Also as we mentioned earlier, try to come to some sort of reciprocal arrangement where you promote your event in association with the paper.

AUDIO AND VIDEO

Another good way to promote your events in a way that gets across your expertise immediately is to give away an audio or video tape of you talking about, or demonstrating, your expertise. Good quality but inexpensive recorders are easy to find today and you can record about 30 minutes worth of material.

It is always a good idea to record your actual seminars and later we will look at more benefits of doing this. But excerpts from such a recording could be put on a cassette tape, CD, video or DVD as a taster for future events.

Remember to include as part of your recordings all your contact details and how people can book to attend. Put the same details on the cover and packaging. As we talked about earlier, include a special discount or incentive for people who book as a result of listening to or seeing your recording.

SMS MESSAGING

Text messaging is still seen as a relatively new form of communication, with the first text message in the UK being sent in December 1992 (source: text.it).

It has done rather well since then with approximately 55 million text messages now being sent *each day* in the UK (source: Mobile Data Association). In March 2003 the figure across all networks in the UK averaged 56 million per day – which is double the number sent in March 2001.

Sixteen-24 year olds mainly use the technology with 95% sending an average of 100 texts per month, but gradually the potential for business is being understood. Many of us have already subscribed to receive regular service texts, e.g.:

- texts from the bank to advise us of our account balance
- information on football scores
- betting tips
- news updates
- weather reports
- traffic reports
- horoscopes
- help to quit smoking.

And according to one survey, 14% of mobile users have even used text messaging to end a relationship!

Whilst text messaging is still a new (albeit rapidly growing communication tool), it will undoubtedly become part of our daily business lives, much as email has (how did we ever manage without it?). Here are some ideas for how it will be used and in many cases already is being used:

- To send short, instant communications such as reminders and instructions to groups of people.

- To convey the same message to groups of people for the same price as sending it to one person.

- To receive advertisements for jobs and vacancies – either from within an organisation or from a recruitment company.

- To communicate with staff in the field or overseas in a cost effective manner.
- To enhance the perception of your customer service.
- To use in a sales situation by targeting business messages at specific groups of people.
- To announce special offers and bargains.
- To announce seminars and workshops.
- To enable people to register their place at a seminar.
- To issue digital, money-off vouchers.
- To announce competitions.
- To build and enhance your brand.

The list is probably endless and only limited by our imaginations. The next logical step is MMS (Multimedia Messaging Services) which, when commonplace will allow us to include video, pictures, sound and music in our instant communications.

As a tool for the seminar organiser, text technology clearly has much to offer and will prove invaluable for not only promoting an event, but in helping to remind people who have booked to actually turn up!

I often use text messaging to follow up a presentation. This has to be done on the same day as your talk to be effective and involves sending a text to all the attendees along the lines of:

'I HOPE YOU ENJOYED OUR TALK TODAY – IF YOU HAVE ANY QUESTIONS PLEASE CALL ME ON (NUMBER). MEANWHILE, PLEASE VISIT OUR WEBSITE AT WWW.TRAININGSTRATEGIES.CO.UK FOR A SPECIAL OFFER (OR WHATEVER). PHILIP CALVERT.'

Just make sure that you put something on your website for them to see! I have also used texting to follow up people who have attended our stand at exhibitions.

'IT WAS GREAT TO SEE YOU AT THE TRAINING STRATEGIES STAND TODAY AND WE HAVE ENTERED YOUR NAME IN OUR PRIZE DRAW. WE WILL BE IN TOUCH WITH THE RESULTS NEXT WEEK! IN THE MEANTIME, PLEASE VISIT OUR WEBSITE AT WWW.TRAININGSTRATEGIES.CO.UK FOR A SPECIAL OFFER. PHILIP CALVERT'

With the latter message you have given yourself an excuse to go back to them again, even if it is to say they weren't the winner and in both messages you have teased them to visit your website. You can adopt exactly the same approach at seminars, either to confirm a booking or to contact people after your event. If you do send 'post event' texts, send them about 90 minutes after it finishes. Texts in business still have novelty value and the recipient will be ever so slightly surprised, but impressed!

In short, don't assume that text messaging is the sole domain of teenagers. There is growing evidence to show that SMS messaging is now growing strongly among more affluent and influential middle-aged mobile users, in particular amongst 35–54 year olds. And as we saw earlier, text messaging is also growing in popularity with the grey market. It is reasonable to assume that this will continue.

PUBLIC RELATIONS (PR)

We have mentioned the importance of using a press release to try to obtain free publicity for your business and your seminars. Whilst one-off releases can be effective, they are more so as part of a planned and structured campaign where you have made the effort to build a relationship with the press over time. Outright promotion of your business in the form of a press release is not necessarily going to get you the publicity you are looking for. There needs to be something newsworthy about what you are doing and generally that means offering something that is seen to be different, entertaining or significant.

This is another reason why I recommend that you take a full five months to plan and put together your events; to give yourself time to build a relationship with the press. You can do this yourself, but there are numerous PR firms who can assist with this important part of your promotion. At the heart of good PR is the ability to communicate the good reputation of a business or individual and this sits very nicely with the objectives behind Seminar Selling – i.e. to enhance the perception of your expertise. You will find PR companies in the local phone book, but The Public Relations Consultants Association can provide you with useful guidance. Don't underestimate the importance of PR – when handled well it can make a huge difference to the success of your promotional effort.

GENERAL CORRESPONDENCE

However much of an expert you are and however good your reputation you still need to get people to attend your event. This means pulling out all the stops. Within the context of carefully planned promotion, it is still important to constantly wear your marketing hat.

Make absolutely sure that your seminars are mentioned in some shape or form on everything that leaves your office or premises. For example:

- If you have a franking machine where the logo and message can be customised, change it to include the title of your seminar, or the date, or the details of a page on your website which has further information.
- If you don't have a franking machine, consider using stamps which reflect your business. The Royal Mail have a wide selection in their Smilers range, and you can even include a photo of yourself as part of the stamp. Buy these in bulk and get known for your creativity.
- Change your fax header content to include a brief reference to your seminars or workshops.
- Print brief details as above on your envelopes, or even make up some stickers which can be affixed to your envelopes.
- Make up a special batch of your notepaper which includes brief details of your seminars. Do the same with your compliments slips.

- Make up some special business cards which highlight your seminar prominently, or add a message on the reverse of your current cards.
- Have a selection of 'giveaways' like pens, mugs, T-shirts, mouse mats, umbrellas, golf balls, coasters etc printed with very brief details of your seminars: e.g. Post-it® note pads can be personalised with your own artwork, photos and designs (see *www.mypostitnotes.com*).
- Have rear window stickers printed for your car with details of your seminars or your website. They are available in a wide range of sizes and designs. They are incredibly cheap and will be seen by literally thousands of people in your local area and beyond.
- If you drive a 4x4 vehicle, you could have a spare wheel cover made up which promotes your company or events. Again, these are generally inexpensive and available in metal, vinyl or plastic.
- Print leaflets about your seminars which visitors to your shop or office premises can take away with them. Include one in every piece of correspondence that you send out.
- Finally, make sure that people who call you out of hours are still given details. Re-record your answer phone message to include brief details, or direct them to either call your mobile phone or to visit your website.

The object of all of this is to *get people to attend your seminars or workshops*. They will only do this though if they can see that there is something of real value to be gained from attending. If they can see that, they will gladly attend and will even pay to do so. So it follows that all your promotional activities must be distinctive and make the benefits absolutely clear. Remember, when someone sees an advertisement of any description which appears to be targeting them, they will subconsciously say 'What's in it for me?'

In short:

- Tell them what is in it for them.
- Spell out all the benefits.
- Offer them an incentive or a discount for booking immediately or in bulk.
- Find an excuse for giving them a discount anyway.
- Offer them valuable bonuses, to reassure them that they have made the right decision.

Above all, get help from other people to promote your events and offer them incentives for doing so.

A great way of getting help is by using the incredible power of the internet.

ONLINE PROMOTION

Websites

If this book was being written in the early part of the 1990s, many in small UK businesses would consider this section somewhat of a fantasy. Yet just a few years later the internet is now firmly part of our lives – to the extent that Internet Service Providers (ISPs) now enable us to keep a live connection 24 hours a day. But as we have seen, the majority of small businesses in the UK are not yet using the internet for e-commerce purposes to anything like the extent they could. Indeed there are some industries in the UK which have yet to grasp the true potential offered by the worldwide web. This is disappointing, but they have much to look forward to!

Your website performs several important functions as part of your seminar marketing activities and considerably enhances and supports your offline marketing:

a. By promoting your main business.
b. By promoting your seminars, workshops, demonstrations, open days and other events.
c. By collecting the names and email addresses of visitors to your site.
d. By enabling people to register for your events.
e. By providing a medium for you to obtain supplementary material for the content of your presentation.
f. By supporting your events by providing *additional information* to that which is revealed at your seminar or workshop.
g. As a vehicle for maximising the profitability of your events by promoting and selling information-based products which supplement your seminars and which reflect your expertise.

As can be seen, the purpose of your website is not just to act as an online brochure, and it's disappointing that so many websites do just that. Yes, it should promote your business, but there is much that you can do to make it an income-generating device in its own right – a bit like an omni-present sales person who is not just telling people about your product, but who is physically working for you by interacting with customers and prospects.

Before your website can become income generating in its own right, you need to get people to visit it. Again, this can be done both offline and online. Offline, you can use all the ideas discussed earlier – just make sure that your website address or URL (Uniform Resource Locator, often referred to as 'Universal') is printed on absolutely *everything* that leaves your building. It still amazes me how many business cards I see that do not have a website or email address on them. I estimate this to be approximately 25% of all business cards I have seen. This is a cardinal sin for small businesses since by not including your email or website address on your business cards and letterheads, you are denying potential customers a way to contact you – and email might just be their favourite way of communicating!

Once people have arrived at your website, you need it to be 'sticky' – and the stickier the better. A sticky website is one that holds visitors for as long as possible and thus increases the likelihood of them wanting more information, purchasing your products or doing business with you. A sticky website will also make people want to return again in future. The principle is the same as in 'real' stores. If people feel comfortable, they will stay longer and return in future.

How do I make my website sticky?

Fundamentally you must have excellent and valuable content, combined with attractive design. Your site must also be easy to navigate and for people to find what they want. Sometimes they don't know what they want, so we will 'help them'. Your site must also be very quick to download or people will leave. Many businesses make the mistake of opting for a site with flashy animated titles. This may be OK for a company which makes flashy animated titles for websites and presentations, but is just plain irritating for people who are looking for information. My advice is keep it simple, high quality and with the minimum of fuss. Think carefully about your use of colours and use a typeface which looks attractive on the screen like Verdana or Tahoma. Be careful with your choice of font, because not all of them are 'safe' or compatible with older software. Times New Roman will be compatible with virtually all software, but whilst it works well on paper communications, it looks old fashioned on websites.

More ways to keep people on your site and to entice them back in future:

- Provide free articles or 'special reports' on your area of expertise. Keep articles to about 500 words maximum and if possible put the first three quarters on one page, with a link to the fourth quarter on another page. This way if the article is of interest, people will be forced to visit another page of your site, where they will find other things to see and do. Special reports 'sound' more valuable so make them available separately as Adobe PDF (portable document format) files. You could also charge for these to enhance their perceived value.
- As just mentioned, give people something to do. Include a poll where you ask a question and provide a choice of answers. After people have made their choice they can see the results and answers given by others. You can use the results of your poll as material for your seminars or for use in press releases. For example: 'Website poll reveals that 77% of people prefer organic vegetables' or something relevant to your business. In turn, this enhances the perception of your expertise and more people will want to visit your website, attend your seminar or request further information.

- Discussion forums, chat rooms and message boards are another good way of making people stay at your website. In fact some people will stay for literally hours! Online forums and chat rooms are not the sole domain of the young. If you are providing a forum for people to talk about their hobbies, interests or business needs, they will use it.

- Include a guest book or guest map. These are the online versions of 'real' guest books you might have at your business premises or home. Your online guest book should encourage people to make a comment about your website, product or service and will give you loads of ideas on how to improve your sales and service proposition. A guest map lets people put a 'virtual pin' in a map so that you can not only read their message but also see where site visitors are in the world. Great fun!

- Include a FAQ (frequently asked questions) page. This is a particularly good tool and helps people to get the information they are looking for quickly and efficiently. It also tells you what sort of information people are interested in.

- Include a site search box. Again, this helps people to quickly find information without having to wade through the whole site. Whilst you want them to look round the whole site, it is better to make life easier for people. At the same time, you will receive regular statistics showing what it is that people are looking for. Very useful.

- Include a site feedback form. Much like a guest book, this feature allows people to tell you what they think of your site and naturally will help you to change and adapt your site as time goes by.

- Include a 'recommend this site' facility. Here visitors can send a brief note to a friend or colleague suggesting that they visit the site. You will be copied in on their details and so can either look out for these people in future or contact them yourself (see 'opt-in email' later).
- Probably the most important thing of all to include on your website (in the top left corner of your home page and ideally on the top right hand side of every other page) is a place for people to leave their email address so that they can opt-in for news and updates by email.

Most of the features above not only keep people busy on your website, but actually help them as well. Many of these tools will give you useful information too and help you to adapt the site to meet most visitors' requirements. Here are a few more ideas which you may wish to include:

- Live news tickers.
- Weather updates.
- Up-to-date financial news.
- Travel updates.
- Daily cartoons and jokes.
- Games.
- Tools for visitors' own websites which you can resell on behalf of professional website developers.
- Classified ads where people can buy and sell their own products on your site.

- Email facilities where people have to visit your site and log in to download their mail.
- Special 'members only' or 'customers only' pages on your website which can only be accessed with a password. The content of these pages may be no more special than what's on the rest of your website, but by providing access with a password you make people 'feel' they are getting something special. Perception is everything!

You may be forgiven for thinking that I have just quadrupled the cost of running your website. If you ask your website designer or webmaster to create all these facilities from scratch, it will not be cheap, but what many people don't realise is that *all* of the facilities mentioned above are available *free* from a wide range of web tools providers. There are even free website templates available that you can download.

The beauty of the internet is that you can get your hands on these tools easily, even if the provider is on the other side of the world. Simply type 'free web tools' into your favourite search engine and get to work! Almost all of the tools are easily customised to your requirements and are provided in code form which you simply copy and paste into the appropriate place in your website. Full instructions are normally provided, together with a comprehensive support service. You can't go wrong – it's that easy. Because the tools are free, you will often find that the provider asks you to put a discrete link to their website, or include a small advertisement. Once you have gained a little experience you will discover how to remove the advertisement from the code or take up the more honourable option of paying a token fee for no advertisements to be included.

Of course this is all very well and good, but it has to have a point. The objective is to make your website valuable and entertaining, but in a way that tells people something about you, your business, your products and service. By creating the right impression on your website (and your offline marketing) you increase the chances of people wanting to attend your seminars.

Website seminar page

One of the most important things to include on your website is therefore a special page about your seminars. The detailed information should not be given on your home page, but should merely be referred to in either the body of that page's text, as a small banner 'advertisement' or within the navigation bar/menu. There's no real reason why it shouldn't be in three places as long as it does not overwhelm everything else. The important thing is that wherever you mention the word 'seminar' it is set up as a hyperlink to your special seminar page.

- Selling your home?
- Searching for the right mortgage?

Like all your other marketing, your seminar page should instantly grab the attention of your visitors by having a powerful headline. It should be in the form of a question, to which you have the answer – an answer which will either make the visitor's life easier, better or which would be of real benefit to them.

The body of the text on this page should be jam packed with benefits and should explain 'how to' achieve or do something, e.g.:

- how to make your house more attractive to potential purchasers so that you get the best possible price, or

- how to get the best possible deal on your mortgage and save thousands of pounds, or
- how to turn your hobby into a profitable business and so on.

If possible, include testimonials from satisfied customers. Once you have held a couple of seminars, you should have some testimonials so include them within the body of the text.

In your text, make sure you use powerful, emotive words and phrases like:

- how to
- discover
- proven
- secrets
- revealed
- we reveal
- easy steps
- special formula
- profits
- you
- free.

But above all, your text should explain specifically how people will benefit by attending. There are various schools of thought on how much text you put on this page and currently the thinking is that you should put too much rather than too little. Like the seminars themselves, aim to give maximum value by providing a high degree of content.

Try to anticipate every question which people may wish to ask and answer them within the body of the text. You may wish to put the text in the form of an interview with you, where all the relevant questions are asked.

We mentioned earlier that it is important to offer incentives and bonuses. Put these towards the end of the page after you have already given people at least three opportunities to click on a link which takes them to your booking form. Some people will go to the booking form/page at the first opportunity and won't even see the bonus that they will receive until they read it all again later (which they will). Remember, the bonuses are really there to confirm in peoples' minds that they are a) going to get high value content at your event and b) to reassure them that they have made the right choice in deciding to attend – so list these bonuses (and their value) near or at the end of the text *after* you have been through the main benefits of attending in detail.

As mentioned earlier, provide people with a wide range of options to find out further information from you or to book tickets. If you are charging for attendance you must also provide a wide range of payment options, including secure credit card facilities. If you do not have such facilities, again these are available from a number of providers and are ridiculously easy to integrate to your site. A popular facility is provided by PayPal and is ideal for businesses which are gradually building their e-commerce strategy. The set-up is free and all you pay is a very small percentage of each transaction (from a little over 2.7%), which is deducted by PayPal at source. PayPal is extremely good value and ideal for small businesses wanting to trade online.

Extra tips to attract people to your seminars

Of course, despite your best efforts, not every visitor to your site is going to find your event completely irresistible, so you need to put in place a few tricks to try to hold them at the exit before they leave.

Assuming you get daily or weekly statistics on your website (you don't?) it is time to start analysing them in detail and using the information they provide. Web stats come in a variety of different formats and at the very least you should be able to see which pages of your site people visit, when and for how long. You should track this information over time to see if there are any patterns and eventually you will see which parts of your site need attention.

For example, make a note of how long people stay on each page and before long you will discover which pages have the least interest to people. Similarly, work out which pages receive the most attention, analyse why and take steps to improve the poorer performing pages. But one of the most important areas you need to look at is the page where people *leave* your site. This is where they have had enough!

Again, try to record the route which visitors take round your site and look very closely at the page from which they leave. Visitors to websites do not necessarily go through a website as though they are following a marked route in a gallery. Despite the best efforts of the website owner, they jump from place to place, from attraction to attraction *as they see fit*. They go to where they think they will see or find something of interest to them, not where you try to force them to go. This is another reason why you should include tools like a search box, or a site feedback form so that your visitors can tell you exactly what they want to see.

Nevertheless, quite apart from good content and design, there are a couple of things we can do to influence their behaviour.

1. Pop-ups

First, the pop-up. Anyone who has ever surfed the internet will have seen these little boxes or mini-websites popping up trying to sell us something. Quite a lot has been written about how annoying they can be, and indeed they can be, particularly if they pop up right in front of something you are trying to read. Some sites have multiple pop-ups appearing where the site owner has sold them as advertising space. These really do cause irritation to many people, in much the same way as unsolicited 'junk' mail or telephone calls in the evening trying to sell double-glazing. We all hate it, but companies still do it. Why? Because it works.

The fact is that many internet marketers will tell you how effective pop-ups (and their close cousin pop-unders) can be – particularly when used properly and in an unobtrusive way. It's a bit like a sales situation where you are not aware that the salesperson has 'closed' you. In fact, they haven't closed you at all, you have voluntarily gone down a path which seemed entirely natural for you to do. No one knows the exact figures, but ten fold increases in online sales are not uncommon through use of pop-ups and this is probably at the conservative end of estimates.

Pop-ups should really be used on either the page of your website where people normally leave, or on the page which promotes your seminar. They should be set to appear only when people click to leave those pages and not before. In addition they should not be any bigger than a quarter of the screen and should appear at the top left.

There are two objectives for the pop-up:

- To convince people that your seminar *really is* worth attending and that if they book today, they will receive *additional* valuable bonuses. These could be free samples of your main product, a free book, or perhaps a free five or seven day email course giving them short tips and advice on something related to your business – but which will be of real value to them. In short, if they book now, they will get even more value.
- The second objective of the pop-up is to get people to leave their email address. You may want to give someone a free 'information product' just for visiting your website, but they can only get it by email so they have to leave you their address. Very shortly we will look at why this is so important.

I have seen some websites where the owner or webmaster has even used a timer which counts down to zero in front of your eyes, and text saying that if you book within the next 12 minutes you will receive even more bonuses. Personally I think this is a little over the top, but at the end of the day it's up to you to decide how you use this very effective tool. The point is though that pop-ups give you a final chance to catch people before they leave your site and to give you yet another opportunity to explain the benefits of attending your seminar or to include a couple of testimonials from previous attendees. When used responsibly and as a natural part of the promotional process, they are extremely effective.

And yes, 'killer software' is available to block your pop-ups, but not everyone uses it and already there are new pop-ups which are not affected by the software!

2. Email and email newsletters

The second thing we can do to influence the behaviour of website visitors is to use the power of email. As we said earlier, we need to try to make sure that visitors to your website are not wasted – in particular local visitors. If they have visited your website at all they will generally be doing it either because they have seen the website address and are just plain curious, or they have stumbled there by accident, or *they are interested in you or the products and services you offer*. They may even have seen an advertisement or leaflet highlighting your forthcoming seminars.

If they visit your website, it would be helpful for you to know this and to be able to capitalise on their interest. In short, they could be potential customers so you need to know their name and get their email address so that you can contact them.

One of the best ways to contact potential clients and customers is through an email newsletter. I firmly believe that in today's world of instant communication, every small business should have an email newsletter as part of their overall marketing mix, if not at its very heart. This can be used to stay in touch with customers and alert them to new products, new services and special offers – and even your seminars, workshops or other events. Email newsletters have a number of benefits:

- You can stay in touch with customers on a regular basis – something a great many businesses are very poor at.
- Existing customers will be quite likely to actually read it.
- It can be modified easily and so targeted at different customers.

- Many people pass on email newsletters to friends and colleagues.
- An email newsletter has the effect of enhancing the perception of your expertise. Good material proves your worth.
- As a sales tool, email newsletters are very subtle and not 'hard sell'.
- They are incredibly cheap to produce and distribute.
- Email is so quick that a newsletter enables people to interact with you. You will find that many people reply with a quick note or comment. If they are favourable comments, ask if you can use them in future marketing materials.
- There is software easily available to monitor 'dead' email addresses and update your mailing lists automatically.
- Newsletters can be formatted to reflect the look, feel and style of your corporate colours.
- They can include hyperlinks to other places of interest on your website or indeed other company websites.
- They can be used to promote your events. If offering people the option to book their place by email, you can give them a custom email address, e.g. *seminars@trainingstrategies.co.uk* or *workshop@trainingstrategies.co.uk*
- They can be income generating in their own right. Your main email newsletter should be free, but you can offer people the chance to upgrade to a more detailed, higher value version if they pay a subscription.

- You can drive people to your website on a regular basis through your email newsletter.

With particular regard to the last point, your newsletter should always contain short articles and information of genuine value to the reader. You should not use your email newsletter for blatant promotion of your products or services. *It is the perception of your expertise in your articles, tips and advice which will make it apparent to the reader just how good your products and services are.*

What makes a good email newsletter?

The trick of a really good email newsletter is to either:

- Keep it really short – just a few lines of valuable hints and tips only.
- Or much longer, but where the first few paragraphs of your article are in the body of the email, with a link through to your website where the rest can be found.

Just make sure that each time you issue a newsletter, there is something new and fresh to be seen on your website. One idea is to run a competition for customers over several months, which involves people getting points for answering questions. Your newsletter will highlight the competition on an ongoing basis and people can check their progress or scores by visiting the website (where they will see something new each time they visit). To prevent potential embarrassment for participants, entrants could choose false names from (say) a range of cartoon or other characters.

If you are going to have a website, keep it regularly updated, but avoid having a label which says 'Last updated: 13 April' or whenever. Unless this date is within the last couple of days, it will always make the site feel slightly out of date.

Making use of your email newsletter

Your email newsletter is also an excellent vehicle for finding material for your seminars. A great way to keep in touch and interact with people is to run regular surveys with your customers and indeed people who are not yet customers.

Ask questions related to your industry and find out what problems people have. For example, a financial adviser could ask clients confidentially what their main concerns are about their finances. You might find that 70% of people say that they are worried about not having enough money to live on in retirement. This will give you a good clue as to what to include in your seminars. Build up a database of problems and prepare solutions accordingly, either for delivery at your seminars, or for written, audio or video form. As mentioned earlier, put your conclusions and solutions in articles for the local press, or write special reports which you give away as an incentive for attending your seminar. You could even sell these reports on your website. Your material and intellectual property is key to the success of your seminars, not just for promotional purposes, but also as a generator of income in its own right. The choice of how you package this information and subsequently use it is yours – the key is getting it in the first place.

People attend seminars and workshops because they want information. Very often that information will help them in some way. If you can find out what sort of problems people have or information they would like in advance, you are then able to make the content of your seminars very much more appealing. And your email newsletter is an excellent way of obtaining that information.

In summary, your email newsletter should be at the heart of your overall marketing strategy as it can achieve so much for you, including:

- Staying in touch.
- Interacting with customers.
- Obtaining information about customers through surveys.
- Using the information to *promote* your seminars.
- Using the information *in* your seminars.
- Selling the information *after* your seminars.
- Driving people to your website where they can find more information (and products).

A few words about gathering email addresses

Unwanted email or SPAM is a real problem which is not going to be solved overnight. The last thing you want to be known for is clogging up customers' in-boxes with rubbish. Your email newsletter needs to be one of the few things that doesn't get deleted without a second glance. In fact you want people to look forward to receiving it. Believe me, if your newsletter is good quality and with excellent content, people *will* look forward to receiving it.

It is essential therefore that people *choose* to receive your newsletter and you can make this easy for them to do by providing an opt-in box on your website or on the pop-up when they leave your website. As we said earlier, this box should be on the top left corner of your home page and you should make it obvious that by registering their email address, people are going to get high value information and advice – in fact anything but junk. This way you make it their choice to receive your newsletter. This is called 'opt-in' email.

Even then, you should send a note back immediately acknowledging their registration (this can be done automatically with Auto responder software) and asking them to confirm that it was they who actually did the registering. Assuming it was and not someone pretending to be them, they will be more than willing to confirm this. This is 'double opt-in' email, i.e. they are given two chances to request your newsletter, thus helping to reassure people that you are bone fide and unlikely to send them unwanted email.

Nevertheless, many people now have SPAM filters which may still prevent your newsletter getting through. Depending on the type of filter software being used, basically it looks out for words and phrases that are typically found in SPAM email, and which are used in a variety of combinations with other words, such as:

- no credit check
- once in a lifetime
- work at home
- unlimited
- take action now
- congratulations
- expect to earn
- additional income
- clear your debts
- free mobile phone
- attention homeowners
- no catch
- dear friend
- financial freedom
- more internet traffic
- no experience
- lose weight
- pure profit

- be your own boss
- compare rates
- stop snoring
- click to remove.

In addition, some filters also look out for too many instances of blue hyperlinks within text.

You can probably guess a lot more words and phrases that are picked up by the filters, but the difference between emails which contain these words and your own, is that SPAM emails are generally trying to get you to part with your money. Your email is unlikely to use many of these words because you are not trying to sell. In fact you are giving – giving valuable information which people have asked for. If you are worried about whether your email newsletter is at risk of being caught by filters, there are a variety of online services which will analyse your text and provide you with a report before you hit the send button.

SUMMARY

We said at the outset of this comprehensive chapter that there are a multitude of different ways to promote your seminars and basically they fall into two types – offline and online promotion.

The key is not to rely on any one type of promotion and to never assume you know how people want to receive information. Try everything and make notes of what works best in your market and for your customers. Where once someone might have seen an event advertised in a letter, on a leaflet or a poster, they can now use another type of medium to obtain additional information and often it is the combination of promotional media which makes the difference.

Provide your customers with incentives to book early or in volume, offer valuable bonuses for attending and make available a variety of different ways to respond to your seminar promotion.

Get people to help you promote your events by giving them generous incentives. Whilst the internet and email are just two ways of promoting your events, they are potentially your greatest 'helpers'. Take advantage of their incredible reach and power.

And finally, whilst I have hopefully given you a few ideas, don't forget good old trial and error!

Having successfully managed to get some people to attend, if you make a good job of the event itself, anything between 65% and 100% of attendees will want a meeting with you. After that it's up to you, but a 65% + take-up rate wouldn't be too bad would it?

> 'I think the most important thing for small business owners to do is listen to their clients. The best thing I did recently was a customer survey. It was done externally and professionally.
>
> 'I gained so many insights from that survey. My clients really opened up and I was happy to get tough messages as well as praise. The insights and requirements helped to sharpen my business strategy. The picture presented by the survey was as important for me to know as the P&L.'
>
> Jacqui Harper MBE, Founder, Crystal Business Training

7

How to Dramatically Increase Your Profits from Seminars

This is where the fun begins and the profits start to roll in!

Most small businesses that run promotional activities and events primarily do it to build awareness – rather than as a means to generate volume sales. Although the awareness and publicity gained may increase their sales over time, the focus of these activities is usually to say to customers and prospects, 'Hey, look, we're over here!' Nothing more.

One of the common problems with small business marketing is that it often does not actually shout 'We're over here – come and buy our stuff!' and consequently is not maximising full sales potential. The little cigarette advertising that is allowed today is not designed to make people start smoking, but is to persuade smokers to change their variety. But small businesses do not have the luxury of a budget to spend on simply building brand awareness. If you run a small business, your marketing spend must work very much harder for you. Ideally, it should **promote** your business, **ask** for business and **generate** business in its own right.

Where businesses do host promotional workshops or seminars, financial gain from the events themselves is not normally the prime motivator for holding them. More often than not, such events are only put on to raise profile **in the hope** of increasing sales at a later date. To make matters worse, many small business owners believe that charging a fee for attendance will actually be a disincentive to people attending. In reality, this is not the case. As we said earlier a **sensible but worthwhile** entry fee will not put off people from attending seminars in the small business market.

PROVIDING VALUE

Indeed, if you are targeting your seminars at larger companies to obtain exposure to corporate buyers, these companies have budgets to attend such events and will think nothing of paying in excess of £250 for a ticket, particularly if they believe that they are going to get real value for their money. And as we have said elsewhere in this book, you must provide real value.

This means that if you are demonstrating your 'secrets' in your particular trade, business or profession, the golden rule is that you must never hold anything back. If for example you make extra special, scented soaps that are known for their beautiful aroma or smoothness or skin enhancing properties, your workshop must 'tell all'. Do not give the audience the slightest impression that you are holding something back from them. The word 'secrets' is used here in a marketing context and gives the impression to potential buyers that they are going to discover something that no one else knows, which in turn makes the product even more special to them.

As consumers, we love to know what goes on behind the scenes, whether it is how the special effects in films are done, celebrities' lifestyles, how magic tricks or illusions are performed and so on. The revealing of secrets is irresistible to most of us and as such can be used to your advantage when marketing your seminars.

TURNING YOUR TALK INTO PROFIT

But the purpose of holding seminars or workshops should not be just to obtain publicity for your business or product. They can and should be used to create and build substantial profits in their own right. And even if you still only want publicity from your events, it is still possible to turn your talk into profit with a little effort.

As we have said earlier, unless you have your own premises in which you can host a talk, you will inevitably have to budget for hiring a venue. But how much better would it be if the event could pay for itself several times over?

In Chapter 6 we looked at how to market your events. In this section we will take it a step further and show how to get even greater value from your marketing spend, to the extent that your marketing effort can create income in its own right.

The really big profits from seminars don't just come from your main product or service that you promote at your events. They predominantly come from **the perception of your expertise** and **your ability to repackage that expertise**. For example, everyone knows that an accountant is an expert on tax, but an accountant who gets on his or her feet, talks about how people **can benefit** from that expertise and who does so in public at a seminar, is deemed to be **more** of an expert.

The simple act of standing up at a seminar has the effect of raising the perception of your expertise. You may not actually be any more of an expert than the next accountant, but **you are perceived to be so**. And of course, perception is everything!

So just hosting a seminar in itself creates an environment for customers and potential customers that is more conducive to them placing business with you. This presupposes that you have half-decent presentation skills and in Part 2 we will show you how not to fall flat on your face when you are up there talking.

The seminar income stream

It's how you use your expertise that determines how much extra profit you will make. Let's look at the income stream from a typical seminar.

Typically a seminar in a good quality branded hotel in the UK with a target audience of 100 people will incur costs broadly as follows:

All day room hire	:	£500
Tea and coffee three times	:	£675
Buffet lunch	:	£1,250
Total	:	£2,425 (VAT included)

This works out at £24.25 per delegate and includes an overhead projector, screen and a flip chart. If you want more than one flip chart, I suggest you go and buy your own so that you can use it again and again. Hire charges for items like this can be extortionate and will severely dent your profits.

Unless you live close to the hotel and can guarantee to be there at least two hours before your talk starts, you should also add on the cost of accommodation for yourself and any helpers. If you feel even slightly rushed or under pressure to get to the venue on time, it will affect you for the first two hours of your talk.

Different hotels will also give you a selection of lunch menus.

Generally you can opt for the cheapest, because if the hotel is any good at all, you will get a decent enough spread to please most people. Unless the lunch is truly awful, it will not make any difference at all to your rating by attendees. They are, after all, attending for the content of your seminar, not the content of the sandwiches.

If on the other hand you are hosting a weekend boot camp, you will have more latitude on the quality of the meals, but generally you will be able to build in the extra costs as people who attend weekend events will pay considerably more for their ticket. More on this later.

So in this example, you need to find at least £24.25 from each attendee to break even. But of course, it's much more than that once you have included:

- Accommodation and meals for yourself and helpers.
- Materials – decent paper and pens (most hotels give each delegate about six sheets of paper and a pencil!).
- Workshop materials – binders, workbooks etc.
- Display holders and stands – to dispense your leaflets and business cards.
- Sweets and mints – bring your own, hotel sweets are dreadful!
- Additional, *new* flip chart pens – the hotel's are always running out of ink.
- A laser pointer, ruler, golf club or similar to point to the screen or flip chart.
- Small prizes for when someone in the audience says something vaguely profound. Offer a combination of sweets and fruit. Whilst sweets are more fun, they can lower blood sugar levels over time,

which can affect the concentration of delegates. The complex carbohydrates within (say) bananas are released gradually, keeping energy levels higher and for longer.

- You may also need to hire or bring your own projector and laptop.

In addition, I give delegates a pad of Post-It notes, a fluorescent highlighter pen and tab index markers. If you can have these personalised with your business name, freephone telephone and fax number, address, email address and website details, then all the better, as they will further enhance their perception of your professionalism.

If you have decided to adopt seminar marketing as a key promotional strategy, then all these things can be budgeted for, but I would rather that my seminars or workshops were purely profit generating, rather than a cost to my business.

HOW WILL WE COVER THE COST OF EACH ATTENDEE?

We have already talked about the benefits of charging an entry fee, so let's now look at how we can pay the seminar bills and generate *additional* income.

To make extra profits, you need to generate extra income and it's fair to say that the normal rules of marketing apply equally to Seminar Selling. That is, if you put on a good show, there's a fair chance that an attendee will want to buy your main product or service. You also hope they will tell a friend, who will in turn attend your next seminar.

Even better is if the friend decides they too want to buy your main product or service. If they like what they get, they in turn will tell someone else, who hopefully will come to a future seminar and also buy your product, and so it goes on. This is called **referral income**.

So the total income from your seminar looks like this:

> Total income (TI) = ticket sales income (TSI) + main product/service sales income (PSI) + referral income (RI)

But we know that TSI above will be £0 if we don't charge an entry fee, and PSI and RI are for the most part unknown (at least for the first few seminars you host).

What we need to do is find even more ways of creating income from your seminars. Here are two.

1. CONSULTING INCOME (CI)

By standing up in front of an audience, you are building an image of expertise. And before I go further, make absolutely sure you really are an expert on the subject concerned, or they will see through you. Better still – try to be *the* expert on the subject.

Whilst the objective of your seminar may be to eventually sell more of your main product or service, there will be some people in the audience who feel there is more to learn from you before they purchase your product, or who wish to hire you as a consultant on a regular basis. This creates your consulting income which is in addition to your main product or service income.

2. ADDITIONAL PRODUCT INCOME (API)

There are huge extra profits to be made through the sale of other relevant materials *at and after* your seminars – either at the back of the room (BOR sales), by mail order or from your website. **But it is BOR sales that are the key to turning your events from merely promotional activity to a high profit generating sales strategy.**

An example of this approach is used in the film industry, where the toys, t-shirts, CDs, gifts and general merchandising of a movie can bring in a massive income on the back of the film itself.

Some business owners, particularly speakers, trainers and consultants find that this aspect of their business becomes so successful that they completely reengineer their business to focus purely on BOR and website sales. Whereas they started out offering consultancy and training, they often move into seminars where they then sell additional materials. In some examples, their sales of additional materials have been so successful, they are then asked to speak for high fees on how they achieve that success. Naturally, they then sell more materials whenever they are asked to speak!

What can you sell in addition to your usual product and service?

The list is endless and only limited by your imagination to create products. Here are some suggestions.

Books

We have said that by standing up in front of a group of people, be they existing or potential customers, you are enhancing their perception of you as an expert.

Assuming you are an expert on your subject (and you wouldn't be in business if you weren't), there is no reason why you can't write down your knowledge. In other words, sit down and write a book. Do your research and find out which publishers want your sort of material, learn how to write a book proposal or synopsis and get on with it. Expect some rejection, but keep at it.

Your own book is one of the best ways of enhancing the perception of your expertise and credibility. People always prefer to listen to experts talking and if you have something in print, it subconsciously tells people that you really are an expert.

Writing a book is probably the hardest way to build an additional product range, but is potentially the most rewarding in supporting your seminars. In time, you may be asked to speak to other audiences on your subject, purely because you have written a book.

The book doesn't have to be published either. You can still bind your document yourself with a spiral binder or in a ring binder. We will see later why delegates will still purchase these items.

E-books

For many people, writing a book may seem too big a step and far too daunting, despite the many advantages of doing so.

Writing an e-book, e-leaflet or e-report is a great alternative and in some cases potentially more profitable. For starters, you don't need to find a publisher, negotiate contracts and so on. You can simply sit down and write about your area of expertise.

The normal rules of targeting still apply in that you do need to do your homework and you can't just write any old nonsense in the hope that someone will buy it.

What is an e-book?

An e-book is an electronic version of something you have written. For example, if you are a financial adviser with an expertise in pensions, you could write anything from one to 500 (or more) pages on the subject, or an interesting aspect of the subject – but preferably including information that people actually want, or think they can't live without.

The information is written using your usual word processing software, for example Microsoft® Word. You then smarten it up, add some illustrations or pictures if you wish and convert it to a PDF (Portable Document Format) file on your computer. Using this superb software from Adobe, you are able to perfectly preserve the look and feel of any document or graphics you have created, be they presentations, leaflets, brochures, spreadsheets or photographs.

The electronic file can then be sent to any other computer in the world, where the text and images will retain the exact look and formatting that you created.

The recipient of your PDF file will need an Adobe® Reader® to open and print the file and this is available as a free download from Adobe's website (*www.adobe.com*).

Within the body of the e-text, you can even incorporate video, sound and live links to websites. If for example you were reading an e-version of this book, I could include a link to *http://www.trainingstrategies.co.uk* on which you can click and be taken straight to the website. I could also prompt interaction with the reader by including my email address. Again, the reader just clicks on the link and your email software is launched ready for use.

As I mentioned above, many of the normal rules of book publishing don't apply. For example, your e-book can be of *any* length.

It could be a two-page summary of something you say in your seminar, or perhaps a checklist to which people can refer when they are searching for, say, an expert on pensions. Naturally, your checklist would steer the reader to your own service. Your e-book could equally tell the reader how to set up their own pensions consultancy and so on.

The potential for e-books which support your seminars is therefore endless and often provides you with the platform to sell information which a traditional publisher might otherwise pass by.

Making a profit from e-books

The best part is the profits. Given that there are none of the normal costs associated with publishing a book (whether through a publisher or self-published), every e-book you sell will make a big profit. Once you have purchased the PDF software, you can make as many e-books, e-leaflets, e-reports, e-presentations etc as you like. As an alternative to purchasing the software outright, currently in the United States it is possible to create an unlimited number of PDF files on-line at Adobe's website for $9.99 per month. They will even give you five free conversions as a trial.

The important thing is that you only ever need to make *one* PDF copy of your leaflet or book. The PDF file sits in your documents file on your computer and you simply email it to the recipient after they have paid for it.

Customers have a variety of ways that they can request and pay for your e-book:

- They can ask and pay for it at your seminar and you email it to them later that day.
- They can email their request after the seminar and send a cheque (or pay by credit card assuming you accept them).
- They can purchase it from your website (more on this later).

As an alternative, some people will feel that they are getting greater value if you can make your e-book available on a CD. Again, this is very easy to produce by copying the PDF file onto disk via the CD creator (burner) on your computer. By doing it this way, the cost of creating the product is only marginally increased, as the cost of purchasing blank CDs is extremely low these days.

To make the product even more attractive, you can create your own covers, again by purchasing some very inexpensive CD cover software online or from your local computer store. Many of these include very professional ready-made templates which you simply customise with your title, name and business contact details.

But as mentioned just now, the key point to remember is that once you have written your e-book or e-leaflet or special report, you only have to make *one* PDF file which is then emailed to purchasers. Now do the maths.

The latest edition (6) of the Adobe Acrobat PDF software retails in the UK for around £249.99 (including VAT). Once you have purchased this and created your PDF files, they can be sold for any sum you wish.

Your e-materials can be sold for anything from around £4.99 for something fairly basic, to anything up to £64 for a much more comprehensive 'book'. If your e-materials are also available on your website, you can potentially receive orders from anywhere in the world and if you want to appeal to the US market you should set your pricing at around $97 US dollars per item.

If you start from scratch today and sell an e-product for £64, you will only need to sell *four* copies to be in profit. If you price something for £24, you still only need to sell *11* to make a profit. Just imagine, if you put on four seminars or workshops over a year to a total of (say) 400 people and sell something to just 10% of the attendees, your total revenue will be £960 at £24 a unit, or £2,560 at £64 a unit.

This works out at £240 or £640 revenue for each seminar or workshop, which goes a long way to paying for the event if you don't charge an entry fee. Think how much extra profit you will make if you charge an entry fee!

If you make your e-books available on your website, the power of the internet opens up your products to anyone in the world.

Consider also offering versions in different languages to broaden their appeal even further. I am currently having some materials translated into Chinese so that they become more accessible to that market.

In short, e-books are pure profit for you. Email is as good as free, so you are not even paying for delivery. And, unless you put your e-book on a CD, you aren't paying for packaging either – because there is none!

What are the key benefits of e-books?

- They are highly profitable (though can and should also be given away free as 'tasters' to potential clients).
- They can include multi-media and live links to other resources.
- They can be read on pocket PCs (and some mobile phones).
- They can be promoted and purchased in a variety of different ways with delivery being automated with Auto Responders (more on this later).
- They provide instant gratification to the online purchaser.
- They enhance the perception of your expertise.
- You can promote your other products within the text of e-books.
- The first pages can be personalised to different clients by editing the original document before converting to a PDF file.
- There are none of the production costs associated with normal publishing.

Tips booklets

Tips booklets do 'what it says on the tin'. They give short, sharp tips that show people how to make effective use of the information delivered in your seminar presentation.

Here are some other advantages of tips booklets:

- In addition to supporting your presentation, they promote your other services.
- They are easy and inexpensive to produce.
- They are easy to read.
- They provide practical pointers on how to use the information that was presented.
- They are perceived as providing added value.
- They can be targeted to different audiences.
- They are often shared and passed between colleagues.
- They can be distributed free or sold for profit as products in their own right.
- Some clients will purchase large quantities for redistribution to their own clients.
- They can be designed and produced in-house using a desktop publishing programme such as Microsoft Publisher.
- They can be made available in 'e form' from your website.

In short, they enhance the perception of you and your company as experts and thus encourage people to purchase your other products and services.

In addition, they have very specific design features:

- They should be able to fit into an inside jacket pocket or standard 11 cm by 22 cm envelope.

- They should have simple but professional design, with very limited use of colours, graphics or photographs.
- The cover should be made of glossy card and bound simply with staples.
- They should have 16 to 24 pages maximum.

Their content is also quite specific:

- The subject matter should be clear, simple and restricted to one area of expertise.
- They should be highly targeted and include very specific tips, facts and help – i.e. no waffle!
- The content should be in plain English, clear, factual and designed so that it can be read quickly.
- They should have plain, straightforward titles that create interest. Many of the most successful tips booklets have 'How to...' or 'Secrets of...' titles. You may not feel that these are appropriate to your business, so adapt them accordingly.

But remember, tips booklets are not a substitute for your presentation or other marketing efforts. They provide support for your marketing messages and should therefore be designed to attract attention, interest, desire and action in their own right. Consider using or adapting titles along the following lines:

- *Twenty-five Easy Ways to...*
- *...Tips for ...*
- *How to Avoid Pitfalls in...*
- *Seven Steps To...*

- *How to Treble Your Sales of...and...*
- *Twenty-five Secrets of Successful...*
- *Revealed – The Insider's Guide to...*
- *Twenty-five Tips to Increase Your Sales of...*
- *Discover Seven Essential...*
- *Twenty-five Tips for Mastering the Art of...*
- *A Hundred and One Ways to Get More from Your...*

Remember – take your product or service and turn your marketing messages into simple 'how to' steps. Don't assume that it will be *too simple* for even your most sophisticated or clued-up clients, customers or intermediaries.

Content continued:

- Try to ensure that the author is a specific person within your business, rather than the business itself. This creates a greater perception of expertise and readers can associate better with a real person.
- Don't put too much on each page – spread it over several pages if necessary to keep it clear.
- Include contact details at the start, end and on the back cover.
- Include relevant references to your website within the text.
- Include one page briefly describing your other business activities.
- Consider including a perforated tear-out reply-paid form for requesting additional information.

Marketing your tips booklet

Depending on your business, your tips booklet can be given away free to support other marketing messages, or sold as a product in its own right.

If the former, expect to give away many free copies. They are extremely inexpensive to produce, so this should not be a problem.

- Send a copy of the booklet with a press release to all relevant newspapers, magazines and journalists. Think laterally and consider new or unusual publications where your booklet may have appeal. David and Jacqui Smith of HomeSmiths Limited near Haywards Heath, UK once advertised in a private school's parent magazine. The advertisement for their upmarket, bespoke home and office furniture cost them about £10 for a year but reached exactly their target customers. So remember – your booklet crystallises the benefits of your main product or service and may well also have appeal to a different market from your usual customers.
- Refer to your booklets in other marketing materials – such as your newsletter, email newsletter and website.
- If referring to your booklet in your email newsletter, include a link to a special page on your website where people can request a copy.
- Produce an 'e-version' which can be purchased or downloaded from your website – in PDF form.
- Produce a version on CD that can either be given away or sold. Again – include links to further information and other products and services available at your website.

- Include tips booklets when making business pitches and proposals.
- Produce a series of booklets and send a copy of just one to existing clients – thus encouraging them to buy more.
- Although your tips booklets are inexpensive to produce, they provide real value. Treat them as such and do not give them away like confetti.
- Within your booklet, include a reference to your email newsletter (if you have one). Encourage readers of your booklet to sign up for the newsletter, which in turn drives them to your website where they can purchase other products or find information.

Pricing your booklet

If you are going to sell your booklets, remember some simple rules:

- The best sales will be immediately after a presentation or seminar. That means *immediately* after – not after the lunch break or by post the next day.
- Have enough available for everyone in the audience to be able to buy one. Have a box full of spares available in case someone wants to make a bulk purchase there and then.
- Offer discounts for bulk purchases.
- Keep the price simple for 'back of room' sales. Never £X.99 or $Y.95. Stick to round numbers such as £5, £10, $15 and $20. This is loose change for many business people.
- If selling your booklet on your website, add postage and packing. Again offer discounts for bulk purchases.

- Both on and off your website, offer customisation (at increased cost) of the booklet.

Do it now! Try this exercise:

1. What is your main product or service?
2. What are the key benefits of your product or service?
3. Who are your customers?
4. Who else could be customers?

Now write down ten tips related to your product or service that could educate and benefit your customers:

1.

2.

3.

4.

5.

6.

7.

8.

9.

10.

These ten tips will form the basis of your booklet for existing and new customers. Now write them again in plain English and then choose a title that shouts **benefits**!

Some more examples:

- *Ten Ways to Save Tax This Year*
- *Twenty Top Tips to Help You Sell More...*
- *The Insiders' Guide to Starting Your Own Business...*
- *The Complete Guide to Investing in Stocks and Shares...*

In summary, use tips booklets:

- to support your presentation and seminar messages
- to establish an image of expertise
- to promote your product or service
- to explore new marketing opportunities
- to distribute added value
- to generate additional income
- to gain free promotion in the press.

Audio tapes, CDs, video and DVD videos

It is important to stress again that it is the content of your seminar that delegates have come to hear. Based on this and the quality of your presentation, individuals will make various assumptions about you and your business and will do one of the following:

- Walk away, dissatisfied.
- Walk away satisfied and informed, but with no intention of purchasing your product or service for a variety of reasons.
- Want more information with a view to possibly purchasing your product or service at a later date.
- Want to make an immediate purchase.

It is important to capture those in the second and third groups by making available additional materials and in a different format. Never make assumptions about how people wish to receive their information, so although you are using one main medium to get over your message at your seminar (a 'stand up' presentation), make other communication media available, even if they have to pay for it.

Audio tapes, CDs, videos and DVD videos fill this role very well and I would urge you to record some of your material for resale either immediately afterwards, by mail order or from your website. We will show you how to do this shortly.

Other people's products

If you are an expert on your subject and looking for ways to increase the revenue from your seminars, I have shown above a number of ways that you can substantially increase the total profits from your event, **primarily using and repackaging your own expertise**.

There is also no reason whatsoever why you cannot sell other people's expertise in the form of their books and audio materials. Make contact with another business person or expert in the same or similar field and offer to promote their products for them. It will be unusual for them to say no and if anything they will be flattered and delighted.

Come to a suitable arrangement with them, and be generous in how much you pay them. I sell a CD and workbook which was produced by Marie Mosely who is a professional speaker, business psychologist and expert on communication in business and we have agreed that I will keep 20% of anything I sell for her. This gives Marie an additional outlet for her product and the availability of her product actually enhances my own seminars.

In addition, by selling other people's products, I am giving the impression that I am more than happy to work with other professionals and am not concerned that my own clients might switch their allegiance.

Finally, if you know of another expert in your field, don't be afraid to promote their events and seminars as well. Negotiate a commission for selling their tickets, and in return, ask them if they would promote your events. This way, everyone wins!

Miscellaneous sales

Other than your repackaged business expertise, it is perfectly reasonable to sell a number of more frivolous items such as T-shirts, hats, mugs, pens, mouse mats, golf balls, playing cards etc. It should go without saying that everything you sell should at least have your website address on it and preferably your name, telephone number, email address and postal address (in that order depending on the space available).

Up to the mid 1990s, personalised printing was relatively expensive, but modern printing techniques have brought the price down greatly.

Always try to have some miscellaneous items available, as you will be surprised what attendees at your seminar will buy, particularly if the event has gone well. If you have put on an excellent seminar or workshop, your coasters, mouse mats and pens fulfil the desire to take something home. Don't **give away** your items at the back of the room, as the souvenir becomes more valuable to them if they have paid for it.

ADDITIONAL POINTS ABOUT CREATING AND SELLING PRODUCTS

Do remember the normal rules about presenting items for sale. Even if they are at the back of the room there are a few things you can do to increase the perception of their value:

- Accept credit cards.
- Price your products at round numbers so that you minimise the amount of time trying to find change. If you have a stampede to your back of room table, you will need a helper unless you can get through sales quickly. I always recommend that you have at least one helper, as many people who make a purchase also want to talk to you – sometimes for long periods of time. You must spend time with them if that's what they want.
- During your seminar, give away a copy of your book or CD as the prize in an easy competition. Ideally, give the prize to someone seated near the back of the room and ask people in the audience to pass it back to the winner. This way, some of the audience get to *touch* the product and glance quickly at the cover and this creates a strong desire to own the item themselves.

- Try to obtain third party endorsements for your books, tapes and CDs and print it either on the packaging or on a board that is visible by the products.
- Offer customisation of your products for bulk purchases.
- Offer discounts for bulk purchases.
- With every product you sell, include a simple leaflet detailing other back of room products that you sell, plus of course details of your main product or service and your website address.
- Think carefully about where you place the table displaying your products. They are called 'back of room' products because they are generally sold 'at the back of the room'. But modern venues at hotels and conference centres aim to make best use of space and you may find it impractical to have your table at the back of the room. At the very least, you want your products to be somewhere that the delegates will walk past – preferably when they are on their way in and out of the room.

  Someone once told me that the ideal place is in the corridor immediately outside the hall you are in – between the coffee and the bathrooms! You will find that even a few inches in the wrong place can kill sales. I once had a table at the front of a lecture theatre right next to the door, so that everyone could see my CDs etc on the way in, at the break and then again at the end. The only problem was that the table had been placed on the stage I was presenting from, a step up of 50 centimetres. Whilst I sold about 15 CDs, the step was too high for many to be bothered to climb.
- Shrink-wrap as many products as you can as this increases their perceived value.

Finally, offer commission to people for selling your products – be they your main product or your back of room materials. You will often find that if you put on a really good seminar, there will be somebody present who is so taken by your message, your enthusiasm and your products that they will be very happy to promote and sell them themselves!

8

How to Create Information-Based Products – Quickly

Not everyone will find that they have the time or ability to create written products, whether a 'proper' book or an e-book. They may also feel that they cannot afford to hire a crew to record and produce a professional audiotape or CD.

However, there are a number of alternatives which can help you to quickly produce high quality additional products to boost the overall profits of your seminar. Most people should find there is at least one method that suits them. Here are some ideas for you.

METHOD 1

As we have discovered, an e-book can be of any length. The word 'book' can be a little misleading unless you really are going to produce a work of significant length and value which has been designed specifically for e-marketing.

However it is possible to produce information-based electronic products with relative ease, which can be sold both at and after your seminars.

First, consider carefully exactly what is your main area of expertise. If you are satisfied that you really are an expert on the subject, next, write down if you have a particular speciality in the subject or are offering something unique.

Write a detailed overview of your topic. This can be anything from two to ten pages.

Decide on 20 to 30 main points that you intend to make and then between two to four sub-points for each main point. Then write two pages on each of your sub points. Before you know it, you will have written around 200 pages.

Make sure it is proof read, checked for grammar and spelling and given a title along the lines of those described earlier (e.g. *How To...*, *Twenty Ways to...* and so on). You may also wish to include some artwork such as photographs, but avoid using lots of different pieces of clip art as this can cheapen the look of your publication.

When you are happy that your document is 'perfect', print it straight from your word processing software, using Acrobat Distiller within your printer options. This will create your PDF file, which you can name and save in the usual way.

METHOD 2

The second method will require you to make two additional purchases, both of which have the potential to make you considerable amounts of money over time. The first time I saw the two items in action I was shocked at the potential they offer to produce information products.

The first item you will need is a digital dictation machine. One suggestion is the DS3000 from Olympus, which can record five hours of normal speech, or two and a half hours at best quality. With the inclusion of an additional SmartMedia card this can be increased to 22 hours of top quality recording, or 44 at normal quality.

Your second purchase will be voice recognition software. Here I suggest the Dragon NaturallySpeaking® software which allows you to dictate at 120 words per minute and produce emails, documents, enter data and even control your desk top by voice. If you are one of those who think voice recognition software isn't all it is cracked up to be, well, things have moved on. If your retailer sets up the software correctly and you are given proper training, you will be amazed at what it can do. Neil Winton at Voice Recognition Systems is an expert on this and tells me that when installed correctly it can even cope with complex medical terms with ease.

The best part comes when you combine the digital dictation machine with the voice recognition software. All you need to do is either sit in your office and record your information, or record one of your seminars on to the dictation machine at the best quality setting.

Then simply download the digital file to your PC and convert it to your word processing programme using the voice recognition software. And that's it! You have a written document of everything that was said at your seminar. Of course, you will need to edit the script, taking out the 'umms' and 'errs' and a lot else besides, but you have at least now got the basics of a document that can be tidied up, converted to PDF and sold as an e-book. It doesn't get much easier and quicker than that.

As an alternative to purchasing the voice recognition software, you could also send your recording to a transcriber who could copy everything manually. Or you could even do it yourself!

If you don't want to transcribe the soundtrack at all, you can use your digital recording as just that – an audio recording. If you want to copy it straight to CD 'warts and all' that's fine. People will still buy it after your seminars if the content is good. And with modern PCs it is now very simple to create your own CDs at home, together with the labels and packaging. Alternatively, your recording can easily be smartened up, with sound editing equipment commonplace in PC stores.

METHOD 3

Another interesting way to produce an e-leaflet, e-brochure or e-book is to recognise that what you are producing is not actually a book in the true sense of the word. And as such it is fun to try different ideas to format the text.

One suggestion put to me by a speaker friend is to record a colleague or friend interviewing you on your subject. The interview would then be transcribed or converted to text using the voice recognition software as before. To give the interview additional credibility, try to find an interviewer who is also very knowledgeable on your subject. Whilst the questions should be scripted, an interviewer who knows about the subject is likely to be more spontaneous in their questioning.

METHOD 4

Finally, if possible I would strongly recommend that you film one of your seminars or workshops, or even hire a small studio. The former is preferable as the film will also show the audience and their (hopefully) positive reactions to your talk.

Once edited and packaged you will have a 'live performance' on tape or CD that can be sold either at the back of the room at future seminars, on your website or by mail order.

This option is the most expensive option, but potentially extremely lucrative. Today there are many small film production companies in what is a very competitive business. Ask to see examples of their work and then negotiate strongly. Make sure your quote includes editing and try to attend the editing session, as you and your material must be shown in the best possible light.

Wherever possible, try to have at least two cameras and opt for the best quality format that you can afford.

Some production companies will give you a small number of free copies of the final edit, but try to negotiate as many as you can, as duplication of your film will cost extra. Remember to have some copies produced in the NTSC format for the United States as VHS tapes don't work there.

WHY WILL PEOPLE BUY THESE PRODUCTS?

In addition to souvenir type products, we can see that it is relatively easy to produce a number of information based products which you can sell immediately after your seminar or workshop, by mail order or from your website.

But will anyone want to buy them, particularly if they have been produced in the office or at home? Surely people only want top quality these days and will not buy something unless there are high production values?

It may surprise you to learn that many of the best sales and personal development tapes that have been available for the last 30 years were either recorded live in front of an audience or in the speaker's study or back bedroom. Many were recorded using portable mono cassette recorders and extremely cheap microphones.

Today we have the benefit of digital technology, which can produce broadcast quality recordings. Even our home video equipment can now produce extremely high quality pictures when used correctly.

The point though is not the quality of the recordings or the packaging (though don't *underestimate* its importance), **it is the quality of the content and material that counts**. I cannot stress this enough because it is the key to making big supplementary profits from your seminars. Whether you sell a video on flower arranging or a Tips Booklet on interior design, it is the quality of the content that will make the difference between your seminars just paying for themselves (if at all) or generating significant additional income in their own right.

So now your total income looks like this:

> total income (TI) = ticket sales income (TSI) + main product/service sales income (PSI) + referral income (RI) + additional product income (API) + consulting income (CI)

EXERCISE

Consider the business you are in, whether a financial adviser, vet, accountant, interior designer, furniture manufacturer, artist, marketing consultant, IT consultant, trainer, florist, gardener, hairdresser, masseur, literary agent, photographer, the list is endless.

Write down three aspects of your work that could form the basis of a seminar:

1.

2.

3.

Write down three information based e-products that you could either sell or give away at or after your seminar:

1.

2.

3.

SUMMARY

In Part 1 we have examined:

- The reasons why seminars should become a key marketing strategy for small businesses.
- How to plan your events.
- How to get people to turn up.
- How to turn your seminars into high profit money-making events.

In Part 2 we will look at how to present your messages with power, impact, clarity, confidence and conviction – because if you can't, do not expect the audience to stampede to your product table to buy your products. You absolutely *must* be able to present your expertise effectively so that you inspire, entertain and inform the audience. If you can do that, they will positively *crave* your products!

Part 2

Getting Your Business Message Across With Impact, Power and Authority

9

Presentation is Everything

Presentation *(n).* 1 the act of presenting or state of being presented. 2 the organisation of visual details to create an overall impression. 3 a verbal report presented with illustrative material, such as slides, graphs, etc.

Spin *(vb).* To present news or information in a way that creates a favourable impression.

To the horror of parents of teenage children everywhere, we live in a world which is dominated by image. Pop stars, footballers and magazines shout at our offspring to tell them what latest gear they must be seen in if they are to be considered cool, chic and trendy. Never mind your personal skills – if you *look* good, that tells your friends everything they need to know about you!

In business too, we are increasingly judged on how our business presents itself to the outside world. We're told of the importance of effective branding so that our business will be instantly recognised or to differentiate our products. We hear how branding will build customer loyalty, increase trust and help to build our customer base. In fact our brand is everything.

This is equally so on the day of our seminar or workshop – only most of us in small businesses do not yet have an established, recognisable brand image that is known to stand for something of value. In fact one of the main purposes of putting on the seminar at all is to start building a brand, because seminars and workshops can be particularly effective at conveying your company's worth and image in the marketplace – particularly at a local level.

PRESENTING AN IMAGE

But are you actually portraying the image you want people to see? How many times have you been to a party or social event where there are strangers present about whom you form an instant opinion – and very often *before* you have even spoken to them? Instantly and subconsciously we make assumptions and come to conclusions on everything from their politics to their trustworthiness. We do it automatically, without thinking. And very often, just as we are often correct in our assumptions, isn't it the case that we are often *entirely wrong*? But by then it can be too late – because first impressions count. Perception is reality.

If it is possible to build an apparently detailed impression of someone across a dinner table who we have never met, just imagine our response to someone standing in front of us who is making a presentation. Particularly someone who, however well they disguise it, is ultimately trying to sell us something! Our senses literally go into overdrive as we analyse every sound, movement and gesture and it's not very long at all before we reach a conclusion, 'I don't like him', or 'I don't trust her'. Some say it only takes 15 seconds for us to complete the analysis process – I don't know, it may be 30 seconds or even as long as 20 minutes. At the end of the day it doesn't matter. **You don't get a second chance to make a first impression.**

Why then is this simple point so often ignored and what can we do about it? Surely we've heard the above phrase countless times before on presentation skills courses or before interviews? Yet working on the skills needed to make effective, authoritative and compelling presentations continues to rank low on the priority list for many in business. Many *believe* that delivering strong presentations is important to achieving business success, but don't exactly go out of their way to ensure that they have the skills to give their best performance.

PRESENTATION SKILLS

Just look at the CVs of many business people under the 'training and courses' section and you'll see 'presentation skills' popping up once every five to ten years or so. Such courses are a bit 'touchy feely' aren't they? For many, there's no real technical meat to absorb and they are really a bit of a skive. Presentation skills courses aren't that difficult to get out of either if you have something else to do. 'I've been talking to groups of people for 25 years, so I think I know how to make a presentation' is a common excuse.

Or is the problem something else? Like the fact that delegates on these courses are usually filmed making a presentation? Good old fear has a big part to play.

In short, presentation skills training is not everyone's idea of fun. Whilst it is intended to help you, it can in fact be extremely stressful, often more so than talking to 500 strangers. But this is no excuse.

Let's get this said straight away. No matter how good your content, **your presentation is everything**. Like it or not, it tells people everything about you, your business, your service, your trustworthiness and your expertise. Your presentation **skills** are the oil which aids the smooth communication of your expertise. And even though the act of standing and talking to a group elevates your position of authority, this image will crash down around you if you are unable to present your messages with clarity, confidence and conviction.

So it follows that if one of the objectives of your seminar is to raise the awareness of your business and its expertise, it is vital that you possess the necessary skills to make it happen. Few of us are born with the skills to present effectively, just as there are no 'born chefs' or 'born accountants' or 'born footballers'. Yes we possess certain attributes which will help, but it takes hard work, commitment and practice to become really good.

Unlike a lot of material on presentation skills, I'm not going to look in any depth at the usual issues – like the importance of not jangling the change or keys in your pocket. What I am including though are my own observations over 25 years of making and being on the receiving end of many hundreds of presentations.

When I ask people what is most important to them when listening to a speaker, the results often prove less predictable than I would have imagined:

- 43% say that the speaker should motivate them to take action
- 28% say the speaker should be passionate about their subject
- 16% say that the presentation should be simple and easy to understand
- 13% say that the presentation should be relevant to their needs
- 0% say the presentation should include visual aids.

I could write another book analysing the figures in minute detail, but the results do support my observations of both inexperienced and experienced presenters at countless talks over many years. And it is the fact that people want to be 'motivated to take action' rather than to be 'motivated to take notes' which interests me most in the context of Seminar Selling.

The whole purpose of our seminars is to promote our business by highlighting and demonstrating our expertise and if it is the case that people want a presentation to motivate them to take action, then all the better! What we don't want to happen is for people to sit and enjoy the talk and then do nothing. It is for this reason that presentation skills are included in this book, so that we can make absolutely sure that our talk *really does* motivate people to take action.

10

Confidence

> 'Believe in yourself! Have faith in your abilities! Without a humble but reasonable confidence in your own powers you cannot be successful or happy.'
>
> Norman Vincent Peale

Hands up who enjoys making presentations?!

Not everyone, that's for sure. There are all kinds of surveys floating about which supposedly show that most of us fear making presentations more than death or flying or spiders or whatever. But presentations are now part of everyday business life. Their value in communicating information or motivating people simply can't be ignored and being competent at presentations is no longer good enough. Despite the internet and a whole host of communication technology, there is still nothing to beat face-to-face interaction between two human beings.

There's something about 'live' performance which is captivating and inspirational when done well. Nothing can beat the buzz in an audience those few moments just before a live concert gets underway – whether rock, jazz or classical. And our heroes rarely disappoint. But what is it that creates this buzz?

Certainly in an audience there is an air of excitement and expectation which is multiplied many times over by the sheer volume of people present. Perhaps it is because we feel we already have a relationship with the band, soloist or orchestra and we're at the concert to enjoy the company of an old friend? Unless your audience is made up of mainly existing customers who know and love your product or service, you are going to have to work hard to create that same atmosphere and buzz. And if that buzz isn't there, you will have to compensate in other ways – so a key element in your presentation is impact.

WHAT ARE THE FACTORS THAT DETERMINE IMPACT IN A PRESENTATION?

There are many things which come into play here, including your content, your appearance, your delivery and so on. But as we said earlier, your seminar actually starts with your first piece of promotional material for the event. Subconsciously people will start to form an opinion about you and your business as soon as they see the first advertisement or the first leaflet or your website. On the day of the seminar itself, the degree to which you make an impact will be determined by delegates very early on.

- Are the directions to the venue clear?
- Is it easy to find a parking space?
- Is the venue attractive and distinctive?
- But most importantly, are delegates greeted personally by the seminar host?

This is one of the most important things I can say about seminar presentations. Make life easy for yourself by building a relationship with as many of your delegates as possible before the event gets underway. Be relaxed, friendly and open with people and shake hands with them. Ask them questions about themselves and on no account look as though you are still setting up or looking over your notes. Now is the time for the audience. Quite often, as part of your 'meet and greet' activities you will pick up or overhear snippets of information about people which may be of use in your presentation or later.

The relationships you build as people are arriving will start to create a buzz of your own – not quite on the scale of the buzz before a Status Quo gig, but getting there! And it's this buzz that will help to create impact for you. Meeting and greeting people in person will also help to build your confidence.

Nerves affect all of us before a presentation and rightly so. In fact for some people, it is a really big problem, but on the plus side, nerves help to tame presenters at the other end of the scale, i.e. those supremely confident people with ego problems! A big ego is a huge turnoff for most people and will do you no favours in your seminars. For most people, nerves actually dissipate after a short while as you get into your stride, particularly if you know what you are talking about. There is nothing worse than standing in front of an audience, most of whom know more about the subject than you!

There are a variety of techniques for easing nerves and building confidence, but the ones which I favour include:

- Stand up straight and let the oxygen get to your lungs.
- 'Act' confidently and authoritatively. As Professor Robert Winston once said. 'Act authoritatively and you will be perceived as authoritative.'
- Spend at least 15 minutes a day for the week beforehand visualising yourself performing well. See the audience smiling and nodding and agreeing with what you are saying. Imagine how you

will feel when they are clapping and talking to you afterwards. The human mind can't tell the difference between something that is real and something that is vividly imagined, so use creative visualisation to help your nerves. It won't just help your nerves – in fact it will actually enhance your performance.

- Smile at people and look them in the eye. You know it makes sense!
- Take a brisk walk outside or around the hotel or venue and breathe deeply.
- Rehearse, rehearse, rehearse and rehearse some more. Do not ignore this part. Ideally, your final presentation should be complete some weeks prior to the event to give you more than sufficient time to become completely familiar with it. Give yourself enough time to completely immerse yourself in your material so that you know it inside out and back to front. Believe me, it does wonders for your confidence.
- Have additional material available in reserve with which to answer questions. You should try to anticipate what questions will be asked, so that you can use this material at a moment's notice. This makes you look very confident in the eyes of the audience, particularly if the questions are asked at the end when it looks like you've already said everything. It will also enhance their perception of your expertise.
- Have a 'proper' rehearsal of the first 15 minutes of your talk – ideally in the seminar room. Like sportspeople, this 'limbers you up' ready for action. If for some reason you can't fit in a rehearsal in the seminar room, try reading out loud for 15 minutes, either at home, or in the loo or your hotel bedroom.

- Don't drink tea or coffee (or alcohol for that matter). Ideally drink water, though preferably not ice cold water.

But above all, the most important thing to remember which will boost your confidence is to focus strongly on the audience and their needs. Just as the key to good salesmanship is to listen and understand the needs of customers, so too should you pay close attention to your seminar audience. Focus on making your talk valuable for them, look people in the eye, observe their reactions to what you are saying and pay attention to their body language. If you have done your research and conducted surveys, your content should already be focused on their needs, but back it up in the way you deliver your material. In short, show and demonstrate you care about them. The switch of focus from yourself and your own concerns to those of your audience makes a remarkable difference in your confidence and consequently in the impact of your delivery.

11

Clarity

'Your audience will be noticing everything about you, so your visual image should reflect the qualities and values you want to project. You may, for example, wish to convey professionalism, integrity and personal warmth. Make sure your appearance is in keeping with these values. Remember too that solid blocks of colour in a suit and shirt, rather than a pattern, will always have more impact.

Tip: Find out what your background colour will be, and then try to wear contrasting colours as you want to stand out from, not merge with, what's behind you.'

Deborah Hall, BusinessTV presenter and media trainer

So you've done your research, you've got a room full of delegates and you've made a great initial impact. Now what?

One of the problems with experts who speak is that their passion for their subject can sometimes be a little overwhelming. Often they have the mistaken belief that their sheer enthusiasm will sweep the audience off their feet. In fact, it may sweep them out of the room if they are not careful.

People are naturally drawn to experts, but it is vital that the passion in their message does not obscure the message itself. Therefore clarity of message is extremely important.

Clarity is important because it aids recall. After all we do want the audience to actually remember what we are saying and ideally, to act on it.

Here are some ideas to help improve the clarity of your message:

- Keep the content relevant to the audience's needs. If you go off at too many tangents, you will simply confuse people. Give them as close as you can to what they are expecting.
- Never assume that everyone knows what you are talking about and *don't use jargon*. Fine between colleagues, but not at a seminar, even if many of the audience have a good understanding of your topic. Use of jargon can also imply arrogance, which is not exactly conducive to building relationships.
- As well as keeping your language so that everyone understands you, keep the overall message clear by only covering one main theme for your presentation e.g. ways to save tax. Within that one theme, try to make no more than four big points with a couple of examples for each. In this example, you could go on to talk about four main ways to save tax, such as through pension contributions, tax free savings plans, utilising exemptions and transfer of assets between partners. Remember, don't get too detailed because the name of the game is to motivate people enough to ask you for more information directly related to their personal circumstances. If you get too heavy, you will only confuse them and they will only be motivated to leave.
- Rehearse, rehearse, rehearse. Another reason why rehearsal is so important is that is helps to 'iron out the creases' in the language of your talk.
- Keep quiet! Don't be afraid to use silence in your presentation to give people time for information to sink in, or for them to ask a question. Silence can be very effective as both a tool to give

people a breathing space and also to build drama and power in a talk. It can sometimes though feel quite disturbing for a speaker to include long passages of silence – even just three to four seconds will feel uncomfortable, but remember, less is more.

- Use repetition. It may sound a bit obvious, but repetition is a great way to clarify your points and there is evidence to show that repeating something a number of times can increase the chances of it being remembered from around 10% to 90%. Quite a lot of speakers have trouble with this presentation technique, because they feel that they may come over as too authoritative if they say something like, 'Let me repeat that…'. But you don't necessarily have to repeat a sentence verbatim over and over again; with practice you can make the same point many times, but in different ways.

- Move about. Movement and gestures can help you to emphasise and clarify points. Presenters very often worry about what they should do with their hands during a talk, but if you are an expert and passionate about your subject, your hands and arms will (trust me) take on a life of their own. Focus on giving the audience value, not on yourself.

- Use humour. Humour can either be very effective or very dangerous! There are a few rules which need to be stuck to. First, unless you are naturally funny and known for being funny, avoid humour. Second, if you are going to be funny, don't tell jokes. Many presenters believe that a presentation should start with something fairly light and so why not give the audience a joke? Yes, as we said earlier, impact is very important, but unless you are a comedian with years of experience telling jokes in front of audiences in smoke filled clubs, just don't do it. You will be no more able to do this well than perform open-heart surgery. Leave jokes to people who are experts in telling jokes.

However, you *are* an expert on yourself, so one way of introducing humour is to say something self deprecating – about your hair, your height, your weight or whatever. This approach saves us all the embarrassment of a joke that falls flat and shows the audience humility which is a very good trait in a presenter.

And even if you are going to use a little self deprecating humour, use it sparingly and above all, rehearse it – many, many times over!

USING DIFFERENT MEDIA

Use different media to support the spoken word. Note 'support'. We will look at use of Microsoft PowerPoint in a moment, but there are a number of other ways you can support your message.

One of the best presentations I have ever seen was by a Swiss gentleman named Rolf Hüppi, who at the time was the worldwide head of Zurich Insurance. On a visit to the UK he addressed the troops for 90 minutes summarising the financial performance of the group over the past year. He spent the entire presentation rooted to the spot and, without any use of PowerPoint, flip charts or slides, spoke with clarity, confidence and conviction. Then, at the most important part of his presentation (which described his vision for the coming five years) took a black felt pen from an assistant and drew about six lines on an overhead projector acetate. He then turned a handle on the side of the projector, winding a clean piece of acetate onto the illuminated surface. After drawing six more lines, Mr Hüppi reached his conclusion and left the stage. It was a stunning performance, breaking many of our 'rules' of presenting, but it was the one, brief use of different media which captured everyone's attention. Simple and extremely effective.

As we have seen, the good old-fashioned overhead projector can still play its part, as can the humble flipchart. Indeed, I believe that these two presentation tools can actually be better at presenting certain types of information than PowerPoint. For example, when conveying statistical information, graphs are often the best way of getting your point across. However, there is nothing to beat graphs which are drawn 'live' in front of the audience. And 'live' is the right word because the act of drawing them brings the numbers to life so that they mean more to your delegates. You do need to practise this approach – in particular drawing the elements of the graph in the *right order* so as to maximise the effect.

For other use of flipcharts, remember to:

- Keep them simple.
- Have no more than four to seven words per line.
- Keep to a maximum of five lines on the sheet.
- Use big writing, preferably in capitals.
- Use blue or black ink with highlights in red.

Finally, if you are speaking in a room which is longer than 40 feet, check before you start your presentation to see if your writing can be seen by people at or near the back.

Finally, magic and illusion is another good way of supporting your message. It should be used very sparingly (unless you are putting on a magic show) and only as a metaphor for something you are saying. It must make a point or it will distract from your message, but when used carefully it can be devastatingly effective. I suppose that it ought to go without saying that its use should always be extremely well rehearsed! If you are interested in exploring this interesting presentation technique, there are a number of business trainers who offer coaching.

A FEW WORDS ON USING POWERPOINT

Remember that the title of this chapter is Clarity. And that is precisely what PowerPoint should be used for. But all too often precisely the opposite occurs.

PowerPoint is now such a magnificent tool that it is easy to get carried away with its fantastic array of functions, leaving the viewer's head spinning in a whirl of colour and animation which the Walt Disney Corporation would be proud of. Whilst the enthusiasm is to be commended, such an audio-visual fantasy does little to help the presenter get his or her message across with clarity.

At the other end of the scale is the user who uses PowerPoint without any of the bells and whistles, but who completely misses the point of using visual aids. As we said earlier, PowerPoint is to *support* your message and can be very effective in doing so. People at presentations remember more of what they see (30% more) than what they hear (about 10%) and the combination of the two can result in people remembering very much more (about 50%). But the effect will be completely lost if the presenter uses the software as a crutch for themselves rather than to enlighten the audience.

Evidence for this is over-cluttered slides where the speaker merely reads the bullet points, overuse of graphs and charts and overuse of clipart. This is just plain laziness and causes audiences to pay more attention to the slides than the speaker. Your presentation is a direct reflection of you and your business and whilst many people *think* that using PowerPoint enhances their image, often the opposite is the case.

As a final word on PowerPoint, I also think that its overuse can create additional unwanted stress on presenters. So much time is put into preparing the slides and animations and worrying whether the technology will work that the speaker inevitably gets distracted from what they are trying to achieve. In other words, the focus stays on themselves and not on the audience where it should be. Presenting to a group of people can be stressful enough as it is, so don't make things worse by giving yourself extra things to worry about.

STORY TELLING

In recent years I have become increasingly interested in the power of story telling in presentations. It is something that good presenters do all the time anyway and often without realising it. We all like to hear a good story and are naturally drawn to people who tell them well – whether with friends, in the pub or at the supermarket. But telling stories as part of a business presentation or a seminar also has very practical benefits, not least of which is the way they help to clarify points in our message. A good presentation technique is to give the audience a couple of facts, which are then immediately followed up with a story. The story provides an example of the facts in the correct context, which has the effect of clarifying the point being made in the mind of the listener. We process stories in a different part of the brain from facts and so this helps us to absorb the material more readily. We also tend to visualise stories in our 'mind's eye' and this too causes us to make more sense of the facts being presented.

This technique is increasingly being used in business as a strategic communication tool. One of the finest exponents of story telling for use in business is Doug Stevenson. Doug has a background in both acting and business and has pulled his experience and strengths together to become an outstanding speaker and coach. He is based in Colorado Springs in the USA, but is often in the UK hosting his Story Theater presentation seminar. Not only is this workshop a fine example of Seminar Selling in itself, it is a fabulous opportunity to discover how to integrate story telling into your business communications. I would strongly recommend it to any small business looking for new and creative ways to increase sales.

In summary, clarity is vital within your presentation. It is so easy to get completely wrapped up in the message you are trying to get across and completely forget the audience. When planning your presentation material, take off your blinkers and get a very clear idea of what you want to say and then brainstorm different ways of saying it.

Don't just assume that you should automatically run a PowerPoint presentation. Are there other, more creative ways of getting your message across which will be more readily understood by the audience? And whatever you do, keep it simple, clear and efficient and think carefully about the image of your business that you want to convey. If the audience sees clutter and chaos, that is the image of your business that they will take away.

If they see clarity, efficiency and someone who cares about them, they will be far more disposed to doing business with you.

12

Conviction

> 'Presentation is everything. But substance and content is vital.'
>
> Rt Hon Margaret Beckett MP

Conviction is an important characteristic of top presenters and conveys the perception of enthusiasm, trust, belief, self-assurance and principle. Although we have mentioned passion on a number of occasions, it is worthless without conviction as this helps to reinforce the perception of your expertise.

Passion on its own can be infectious, but it does not work for everyone in an audience and each attendee at your seminar or workshop must believe that you are sincere as well. Conviction is something that you either have or you haven't and it could be argued that it is something you can't train into people. Nevertheless, presenters should be aware of its importance.

There are several characteristics of good presenters who display conviction.

- Presenters with conviction rarely appear to be 'selling' their product or service in their presentations. Their enthusiasm and expertise is apparent to all and this is usually sufficient to convince attendees of the quality of your main product or service.
- Presenters with conviction are skilful at pitching the level of expertise at just the right level with audiences. They appear to be able to read audiences well and neither patronise them nor go too far over their heads.

- Presenters with conviction will make minimal use of notes. Notes, while being useful, are really a crutch for the presenter and those who know their subject well (and who have bothered to thoroughly rehearse) will be less likely to use them to any great degree. Again, the amount you use notes or a script will influence the audience's perception of your expertise.

- Those who do not use notes and scripts usually adopt a more conversational tone in the delivery of their presentation. This makes them look more 'human' and more authoritative – something to which audiences are inevitably attracted.

- Look people in the eye (more on this in Chapter 5). There are various schools of thought on where you should look when addressing an audience. Some trainers say you should find a spot at the back of the hall or room and use that as a 'marker' so that your voice will be clear to everyone. I tend to take the view that if you care about each and every member of the audience, you will make every effort to address each one of them. There is no better way in my book than by looking people in the eye – and for that moment speak directly to that person.

  None of us trust people who don't look us in the eye when they are talking to us, so why should it be any different in a presentation – particularly one where the presenter is trying to convince people of their expertise?

- When using stories as part of a presentation, try to use examples from your own personal experience and ideally stories of personal adversity. Again this creates an image of humility and gives extra credibility to your message.

We can all think of examples of television personalities who are really passionate about their subject and although they are people who are occasionally considered as perhaps less glamorous, cool or sexy than some other celebrities, they are often felt to be much more sincere. Love or hate the never ending conveyor belt of cookery programmes, you can't fail to be impressed by the celebrity chefs' technical expertise, dedication, confidence and heartfelt belief in what they do.

Perhaps Mrs Beckett's quotation should have been: 'Presentation is everything. But substance, content *and conviction* is vital.'

13

Connection

> 'We can only connect through trust. People trust referrals from other people who've had a good experience with your organisation. Following recent scandals such as Enron, Worldcom and Andersen, most organisations are rightly focusing on a psychological turn-around. They are spending time developing trust with their staff, customers and suppliers.
>
> How are you building trust? What are people saying about you? Do you know? Is it contributing positively or negatively to your organisation's success?'
>
> Marie Mosely, Business psychologist, international speaker and broadcaster

Connecting with members of your audience or group is about chemistry and relationships. The two need to go hand in hand.

However, relationships need to be worked on and nurtured, but unfortunately for you, unless your seminar has an audience made up of close friends and family, you will have a lot of work to do to get the relationships up to speed quickly, so that people will be interested, excited and ready to hang on your every word. We mentioned earlier the importance of meeting and greeting every attendee and this is the first step in this very important relationship building process.

As well as introducing yourself, try to introduce people to each other so that conversation builds. The sound of conversation in a room when people arrive helps them to feel more inclined to participate, as the last thing you want is silence. Background music on arrival also helps to relax people and make them feel welcome (remember – you need a licence to do this).

Make sure that everyone has a badge with their name and if appropriate, the name of their business. You will find this is of as much benefit to you as them, particularly when making introductions. Ask one of your helpers to stand behind the registration table to welcome people and give them their badge. Lay out the badges on the table with the names *facing the helper*. You want the badge to be found as quickly as possible as this helps people to feel that they are expected. The delegate will still spot their name even if it is upside down, so together with the helper viewing them the right way up the badge will quickly be found.

Treat the period when people are arriving a bit like a cocktail party – get them talking and interacting. All your focus should now be on them and under no circumstances should you concern yourself with projectors, flipcharts, notes or any of the other mechanics of your presentation.

We discovered that a little light humour directed at yourself will also help to oil the wheels. The warmth you create during this opening 20 minutes before your presentation is crucial to the degree to which you connect with people when you start talking, so make sure you put in the effort so that they are as receptive as possible to you.

GETTING STARTED

When your seminar starts, try to have someone else introduce you. This is not vital, but it does help to build your credibility right from the start and set the right atmosphere. It doesn't matter who does the introduction for you, just as long as you give them a script, and that they practise reading it for several days beforehand. It also doesn't matter if they read it when introducing you and because they probably will read it rather than learn it, print the introduction in large, clear type. The script shouldn't be too long, flamboyant or include too many of your achievements – just a few well-chosen words to start things up.

Whilst we agree that impact is vital at the start, concentrate on making a *friendly* impact. Feel free to burst on to the stage like the Rolling Stones, but ensure you make an impact for the right reasons. You must be seen at this early stage as friendly, personable and approachable, so that people subconsciously think 'I like this person'.

Here are a few more ideas to help you connect with the audience:

- Walk with purpose and look positive and optimistic.
- Actively listen to people when they speak to you on arrival. Look them in the eye and *really listen hard.*
- Don't stand behind a lectern at the early stages (ideally, don't stand behind a lectern at all!).
- Ask people at the back if they can see and hear you.
- Ask people if they are too hot or too cold.
- Reassure people that they can get up and move about if they are uncomfortable.

- Make an observation about something local that they would have heard about – like the new traffic lights down the road, or the weather.
- Tell the audience that you have been looking forward to the event.
- When someone asks a question, repeat it for the benefit of the room and then answer it to the whole room. When you have finished answering the question, ask the questioner if that helped them.
- Above all, smile.

At some seminars, particularly events that last several hours, the host will (not surprisingly) arrange for an additional speaker to make a contribution. In many ways this is good as it provides added value for the audience. On the other hand you run the risk of them being a better speaker or more charismatic than yourself. The worst-case scenario is that the audience perceive the other speaker to be more of an expert than you. This could result in people gravitating to the other speaker at the end of the event and worse still, buying that person's back of room products instead of your own! As we have said before, the whole point of seminars and workshops is to provide a forum or platform for you to demonstrate your expertise. You don't want your seminar becoming a platform for someone else.

STAYING CONNECTED

Staying connected with people is just as important. Make sure you have regular breaks, whether it is for tea, coffee and comfort breaks or even for people to get some fresh air. Some people will want anything but fresh air, but whatever the reason, stop and let people out regularly.

When you are dealing with a complex part of the presentation, perhaps involving numbers or statistics, try to keep these passages short. After any period which has needed intense concentration, immediately follow it with either a formal break or lighten things up considerably by changing your tone, pace, moving about, saying something amusing (about yourself) or completely changing the subject. In fact regularly changing the pace and tone of your talk is to be recommended anyway as it helps to keep people awake and alert.

However passionate you are about your subject, don't ever get to the point where you run the risk of irritating people. Most will be impressed with your knowledge and expertise, but do allow room for other people's views. After all, they have decided to attend your seminar because they have an interest in your subject, so it is very likely that they will have their own thoughts and ideas. Even if you are the world's leading authority on a subject, always listen with interest and respect to what people in your audience have to say, and never argue – even if they are irritating you!

Equally, do not ever underestimate your audience. There are always people present who know more about the subject than you think. If you ever talk down to them you're in for trouble.

AFTER THE EVENT

It is just as important to keep the connection going immediately *after* your talk as before and during it. If you have back of room products, this is the point when you need to be at your most charming. Even if people have already decided that they will purchase your book or tape or whatever, it helps to reassure them of the wisdom of making the purchase if they can briefly talk to you in person. You may even find that they would like it signed. Write their name in the book as well, but check the spelling first.

Sometimes you will find a queue of people waiting to talk to you. For this reason it is useful to have helpers who can sell your products for you. Although you want to sell products, it's important that you spend time talking to people – some will want to talk for 20 minutes or more! You must still be seen as friendly and approachable as this is something that people will tell all their friends and business associates about.

Part 3

What Happens Next?

14

Getting Feedback

'My entire perspective on the business of sales and marketing is coloured by my being transgender.

It amazes me how as a man I failed to see just how little attention businesses pay to the fact that a significant growing number of their buyers are women. 85% of consumer payments are made by women, 45% of the workforce are women, marketing and buying departments are predominately staffed by women, 40% of new businesses are owned by women.

Yet most advertising and marketing is based on male communication strategies. To succeed in sales and marketing in the next decade small business owners will need to look hard at how to reach their female buyers.'

Rikki Arundel, Professional Speaker, GenderShift.com

So you have reached the point where the big day has come and gone. And hopefully you will already have won new customers. They may be customers for your new back of room products, or your main product or service. You may even have had people ask you to provide high value consultancy services.

You should also have found new friends who will be great advocates for your business and who will be busy spreading the word about your seminar or your expertise. You will also find that more people will be visiting your website where they can find out more information about your main products and services.

This is all fantastic news, but it's important now to be thinking of the next step and looking for ways to improve both your content and delivery for future events. The best way to do this is to ask the attendees, from whom you will obtain both formal and informal feedback.

FORMAL FEEDBACK

The best way to obtain feedback from delegates is to ask them to complete a post-event questionnaire. This should be given to them on the day as part of your closing comments. Keep to just one side of a sheet of paper and ask questions which provide you with practical advice with which to improve the event. It is always nice to have comments which say how good the event was but you should be thinking to the future. Include by all means questions which will produce responses which could be used in future marketing materials, but focus on improvement. You also want these attendees to help you with the marketing for your next event, so ask them to include the names of other people they know who might benefit from this seminar or workshop. Wherever possible, try to get their email addresses.

As well as giving you referrals for future events, you can also ask if people would be interested in helping you to promote future events as an agent or affiliate of yours. Make it clear that you will reward them for their efforts.

Your questions could include some or all of the following:

- How, specifically, have you benefited from today's seminar?
- How will you use the information you have been given?
- How will the event affect your productivity?

- How could the event be improved for the benefit of future attendees?
- What would you include that was not covered today?
- Was there anything that should have been left out?
- Which was the most enjoyable or useful part of the presentation?
- Was there anything that was unclear?
- Was there anything of particular interest on which you would like further information?
- What comments do you have on the venue?
- Was it easy to locate?
- Is there a different venue that would be preferable to you?
- Were there any problems that we should be aware of in future?
- Was the time of the event convenient for you? Do you have any suggestions in this regard?
- To what extent would you recommend this seminar to friends and colleagues?
- Are there any products or services which we currently do not offer, which could be of use to you in future?
- Please would you provide the names of three people who you think we should approach?
- What is the best way to contact you so that we can send any updates or supplementary information?

As you can see, all these questions are designed to illicit information which can be used to your benefit. You may also want to include a final question which asks attendees to write a general comment on the day. As was the case on all your promotional material, remember to include your email and website addresses on your feedback form. Although most people will hand it in there and then, some do not so you need to give them another chance to send it back separately.

If anyone asks a question on the post event form, make absolutely sure that you reply immediately. A week afterwards is too late – try to make it the day after your talk.

Your formal feedback is vital – just make sure that you use it.

INFORMAL FEEDBACK

Informal feedback is made up of snippets of information that you pick up on the day of the event both before, during and immediately afterwards. Keep a notebook with you on the day to write down anything that is said to you or that you overhear. Make a note too of the questions that people ask so that you can be better prepared in future. If you have helpers with you ask them to also keep notes of anything which came to mind.

Put a shortened version of the feedback form on your website to enable people to make any comments or additional points. This should be included on a special page which only attendees can visit. On the day of your event, give people a note of the address of the special webpage and explain that only seminar attendees have access to it. Set up the page so that it requires a password to access, and make a point of giving out the password to people in a sealed envelope at the end of the event. By offering a special webpage you make your attendees feel special and the sealed envelope adds an extra air of mystery.

Also on this page there will be a summary of the topics covered in the seminar (even though they will have been given a workbook or have taken notes), together with supplementary information. Provide choice in the way people can feed back information through your website by giving both an email address they could use (e.g. *seminarfeedback@trainingstrategies.co.uk*) and a form with boxes they can fill in.

The special webpage needs to be live on the day of the event itself as some people will go straight back home and immediately log onto your site.

SUMMARY

If you have had a number of helpers or colleagues involved in your event and they are all present on the day, aim to have a debrief meeting within half an hour of the last delegate leaving.

You will all, I assure you, be extremely elated and tired. Very tired! But it is your first impressions that really count. Your tiredness will help you to remember the things that did not go well or which needed improvement and your elation will help you to recall what went well. Write down your thoughts and add them to the information gained through the feedback forms, your notes and any comments which come in via your website.

As a final point, consider asking five delegates if they would be interested in providing more detailed feedback. Choose a cross section of attendees and ask if they would be willing to either complete a more detailed feedback form or take part in a one-to-one interview with you where you go through each section of the event. In some cases you might wish to consider filming or recording these interviews as they will help you to remember the detail later. With permission, you may even be able to use snippets of the interviews in future marketing materials or include them on a recording of the event itself for later sale.

Yes – even your feedback can be turned into profits!

15

Following Up to Maximise Sales and Profits

> 'Word-of-mouth marketing is the easiest and most cost-effective way to increase sales. We are a gossip species. Human beings talk about each other. When we encourage those we know to do it proactively, we dramatically increase the effectiveness of word-of-mouth marketing.'
>
> Roy Sheppard, International Speaker and Moderator
> Rapid Results Referrals

There really is no point running seminars and workshops unless you follow up afterwards. You have gone to great lengths to put on a high quality, high value event which will hopefully have impressed your delegates or attendees.

You will have gathered some useful feedback and will already be working on your next event. But now is the time to pull it all together.

Following your debrief meeting you can go to the bar to relax. You deserve it. But the next day you have work to do.

THE NEXT DAY

Just as you have planned the content and promotion of your event, you should also plan your follow up. Remember to refer to your overall objectives for the events and plan the follow up accordingly. Decide exactly what you are going to do to follow up and when.

One thing you must do is to send out pre-prepared follow-up letters to each attendee. Allow room to add in any special remarks which reflect anything particularly interesting or amusing that happened or was said during the day. Also, find the answers to any questions which you were not able to answer. It is very important to answer questions immediately as this adds to your credibility. It would be even more impressive if you were able to send out these letters on the day of the event itself so that they arrive the following morning. This is normally quite difficult to achieve, but well worth it if you can manage it. Include a handwritten 'PS'.

A novel and distinctive approach is to send a follow up text message on the day of the event. Naturally, keep it short! You'll be surprised just how many people will respond.

Contact anyone who was not able to attend and send an appropriate letter. Offer them a further incentive to either attend a future event or a discount on your products (either back of room or your main product). You may even wish to give them access to the special web-page complete with the relevant password.

On the day of your seminar you will have told all your attendees that you are holding a draw for everyone who attended. Pick the winner the next day and personally deliver the prize.

Send a press release to the local papers summarising the event but write it in a way which explains how attendees benefited and include information about future events which you may be holding. Ask one of your helpers to take a photograph of you at the seminar and include it with your release.

If you filmed or recorded your seminar, now is the time to be editing and packaging your video, DVD or CD. Ask your webmaster to use clips on your website which visitors can watch or listen to.

CLOSER ANALYSIS

As part of your follow-up process you will be analysing all the feedback from the event and starting to take the necessary steps to make improvements for next time. The feedback is important as it could directly impact the profitability of future events.

Typically analysis will reveal problems as follows:

- Not giving enough time to the planning of the event.
- Not having clear objectives that are written down.
- Not targeting the content of the event at the needs or problems of attendees.
- Not promoting the event in a broad enough range of media.
- Not providing sufficient options for people to make further enquiries or to respond.
- Not providing sufficient incentive to attend.
- Not highlighting sufficient benefits of attending.
- Not making the event irresistible to people in your target market.

During the event, analysis of feedback will reveal:

- Equipment failure.
- Overuse and poor use of PowerPoint.
- Not being sufficiently friendly, relaxed, enthusiastic, cheerful or inspirational.
- Lack of rehearsal.
- Not providing what was advertised.
- Holding back the ‘meat’ of your knowledge and expertise.

- Lack of attention to maintaining a strong connection with the audience (i.e. building relationships and keeping them alert at all times).

After the event a common problem is not following up on promises made during the presentation. If you tell someone that you will get back to them with an answer to their query make sure that you do. Nothing is worse for denting your credibility.

MAXIMISING SALES AND PROFITS

As time passes and you have held several events you will develop your own ways to plan and prepare your events. You will discover your own ways of promoting the events and the best ways of doing so within your target market. You will also be building an impressive list of contacts who have opted-in to receive details of additional products and services.

Just as your seminars do not seek to overtly promote your products or service, neither should your follow-up activities. Your promotional activities should always aim to highlight your expertise, from which prospects can draw their own conclusions.

Your email newsletter should be at the heart of your follow-up activities, by providing regular, valuable hints, tips and advice for people interested in your business. The newsletter must provide real value or it will soon be consigned to the recycle bin. It has four main objectives:

1. To keep in touch with your customers and prospects.
2. To drive people to your website.
3. To remind people of your expertise and the quality of your service.

4. To advise people of future events.

1. Keeping in touch

Not keeping in regular contact with customers and prospects is a common problem in business. It is, in fact, unforgivable and in today's electronic age completely unnecessary. Scheduling in time to contact customers is vital and email is particularly effective for doing this.

The trick is to keep your email newsletters short and full of value. Even though your recipients will have asked to receive your newsletter, they still don't want too much to read. If they want more to read they can click through to your website.

2. Driving people to your website

For people who attend your seminars you want your website to act as an alternative place to experience your business. You can use this piece of cyberspace to build on ideas in your newsletter and to provide additional information not covered at your seminar. For those who attended your seminar, your website gives another opportunity to promote your back of room products, in particular your information-based products which can be sold in electronic format. As we said earlier, e-books can be extremely profitable as they only need to be produced once. A number of professional speakers sell e-books on their websites and use their email newsletter as their main promotional method. Many will tell you that someone needs to visit your website four to six times at which point they will purchase a product online. And there is evidence to show that the same person will visit your website again in the month following and will make another purchase. So you can see that if you have a tool that is encouraging people to visit your website on a regular basis, there is a strong likelihood that this will pay dividends. Don't forget, each e-book you sell is pure profit.

It's quite one thing for someone to visit your website and to see details about an information product that you have written. But unlike books in a bookshop you can't pick them up, touch them, smell them and read a few paragraphs, so how do you expect people to be attracted to them? Again, this is where your seminar comes in. People who have seen you 'live' and witnessed your expertise at first hand will have been given all the information they would ever need to decide whether they want to buy your e-book. Similarly this is another reason why your email newsletter has to be of high value. People will have already read a great deal of your work and will have come to their own conclusions about the likely value of your product.

But a great way to reinforce the message is to give your e-book a 'real' cover. Software is available for you to design a sleeve which can then be put on your website. It actually looks like the cover of a real book, complete with your name and title and so enhances the perceived value of the product. To make your e-book look even more 'real', the software creates the cover in 3D to make it look as though it is standing on a shelf.

3. Reminder of your expertise

Assuming you delivered high value and high content at your seminars, your email newsletter will help to reinforce your expertise. But it must at all costs be worth the virtual paper it is printed on. If your recipients are satisfied that it is of value to them, you will have a friend and very often, a customer for life.

These recipients will buy your products, participate in surveys and competitions and will even travel long distances to attend your talks.

It is also the case that not everyone who attends your seminars or workshops wants to buy anything at all from you! But they just might in future, so you want to make sure that when they are ready to buy something they come to you first. It is possible for many recipients of your email newsletter to stay quiet for months or years without ever communicating with you. It doesn't mean they don't read or enjoy your communications – just keep in touch and one day that call will come.

You will also recall from earlier in the book that you can make money from the email newsletter itself by offering a 'premium' version which people have to pay for. Naturally the content will be of even greater value and you will find that a great many of your 'fans' will be more than happy to upgrade. Apart from anything else, the curiosity alone will have its appeal.

4. Information on future events

As well as profits from your seminars themselves, consultancy activities, back of room products, website/e-book sales and email newsletter upgrades you also have the option of advertising future events and offering Premium Seminars.

Sometimes known as boot camps, Premium Seminars take your events to the next level. They provide you with a platform to offer a workshop for those clients or prospects who are looking for more exclusive, higher value material which is perhaps more appropriate to their needs. Such events are often held over a weekend at a prestigious and comfortable venue and invariably will be at a price which reflects the quality of the event. Given the location you may also want to include a more social aspect in the agenda and schedule in time for delegates to make use of a variety of leisure facilities. Not surprisingly, if you charge anything from £300 upwards the profits from these events can be substantial, particularly if you have a wide range of back of room products available for purchase.

SUMMARY

On several occasions throughout this book we have talked about the benefits of email newsletters. Fundamentally their main value is in providing the small business owner with an inexpensive, quick, interactive, easy and efficient communication tool which can be used to not only provide information to customers and prospects, but to rapidly direct people to additional information.

Email is unrivalled in its ability to perform a variety of communication functions and whilst unwanted email can be a big problem, when used carefully, correctly and creatively it can be an extraordinarily powerful business tool. I urge you to explore its possibilities.

Some Final Thoughts

So there it is – a new promotional strategy for your business. Only it's not that new!

Demonstration-based selling has always been extremely effective because it allows the prospect to see your product or service in action before they get out their wallet. But it is not just the demonstration that makes the difference. It's the ability of the prospect to go to a deeper level and gain a more detailed impression of the people behind the business.

Today's consumers are much more sophisticated than they were even a few years ago and with the advent of the internet they are now able to compare hundreds of different products from the comfort of their own home. Indeed, the detail in which they can compare products is staggering. Every tiny piece of information that you might want is available immediately, and even if it isn't, it doesn't take long to find it.

Not surprisingly, many products are increasingly being commoditised as customers can not only compare product features, but can quickly locate stores offering the lowest price.

So how do small businesses fight back?

Service is an obvious differentiator, but many businesses struggle to find ways of making their service both creative and innovative. Even more difficult is to convince customers in a leaflet or on a website that their service really does offer something special. After all, every brochure from every business in every part of the UK claims to offer service which is 'second to none'.

How then can we *prove* to people that we really do have the edge and that we truly surprise and delight our customers?

By showing them. By giving them a live demonstration of our expertise. By enabling customers and prospects to see, touch and experience what we do at a seminar, workshop, demonstration or social event. What better way could there be to promote our product or service?

Businesses have always hosted these events and those that do know all too well how effective they can be. But far too many do not and they are missing out. It's easily understandable why they do not, but I hope that this book will give them a few ideas. The good news for them is that effective Seminar Selling is not just about putting on a nice talk and then waiting for the orders to roll in. When combined with today's incredible communication technology the possibilities are endless. But it is the way that technology can be employed to market, support and follow up your events which is most exciting. Not only that, the very same technology that you use to promote your events can be used to create information products and produce incredible profits in their own right.

Successful Seminar Selling is a magical combination of substance, style and good old-fashioned face-to-face communication skilfully blended with modern communication technology. It gives you a golden opportunity to stand out from the crowd and show customers what your business is really all about.

Grasp that opportunity with both hands today.

Good luck with your seminars, workshops and demonstrations – in fact *all* your promotional activities. Let me know how you get on!

Successful Seminar Selling

Five-month Countdown to Winning More Business

	PLANNING	INITIAL PREPARATION	PROMOTION	FINAL PREPARATION	PERFORMANCE	POST PERFORMANCE
5 MONTHS TO GO	- Decide to hold seminars – one-off or a series - Decide objectives of seminars - Decide subject matter - Decide target audience: prospects, existing clients or both If inviting existing clients, allow in numbers for them to bring a friend - Decide whether to use a professional meeting planner - Decide whether to involve a PR consultant, or write a PR plan - Decide: free or charge for entry - Decide provisional dates, check for industry exams & other clashes etc. Avoid holidays, Mondays and Fridays - Decide on numbers to invite - Decide on incentive to attend - Decide who should speak, and invite any other speakers verbally - Make enquiries about any available funding or subsidies - Decide event budget	- Write marketing plan – include and consider all possible means of communication, including: ◆ Advertising ◆ Email ◆ Fax ◆ Mail shot ◆ Mail drop ◆ Text messaging ◆ Radio advertising ◆ Personal letters ◆ Newsletter ◆ Telephone - Include all possible methods of response: ◆ Email ◆ Coupon (freepost) ◆ Phone (free) ◆ Fax (free) ◆ Text ◆ Website form ◆ Website link ◆ Website pop up - Check out (ideally visit) venues and prices - Provisionally reserve venues - Design promotional stand or pull-up banners				

	PLANNING	INITIAL PREPARATION	PROMOTION	FINAL PREPARATION	PERFORMANCE	POST PERFORMANCE
4 MONTHS TO GO	- Decide if you are going to sell any products at the event - Consider designs for any promotional sales items	- Write first draft of agenda - Write second draft of agenda - Design tickets; include endorsements - Consider any corporate gifts - Decide how people can pay for tickets ◆ Online ◆ Cheque ◆ Credit card (arrange merchant account if necessary) ◆ Standing order for several events - Write email mailshot - Draft leaflets for inclusion in mailshot – proof read - Draft PDF of leaflets - If selling any written products get writing or bind copies of articles you have written	- Start PR activities to build relationships with local press	- Confirm dates with additional speakers - Confirm, arrange and book radio advertising - Confirm hotel bookings - Arrange printing of tickets - Arrange printing of leaflets - Arrange corporate stand and banners - Arrange any corporate gifts - Create PDF leaflets - Arrange printing of promotional sales items		

	PLANNING	INITIAL PREPARATION	PROMOTION	FINAL PREPARATION	PERFORMANCE	POST PERFORMANCE
3 MONTHS TO GO	- Start planning for follow-up seminar if running a series	- Decide if the event is to be filmed or recorded and agree promotional strategy - Contact production companies - Write first draft of event programme – proof read - Write first draft of your presentation - Determine equipment needs for event, and special needs of speakers	- Send personal letter to existing clients - Write info for newsletter and proof read - Update website - Send out mail shot - Send out email shot - Send out newsletter (attach handwritten Post-It note) - Leaflet drop to target residential areas - Draft and send press releases - Continue PR activities	- Confirm advertising space with appropriate newspapers and magazines. Ask for a spot early in the publication on a right hand page - Acknowledge first wave of bookings - Remind other speakers to allow plenty of time for preparation - Confirm equipment needs - Write final draft of the agenda - Set up answer machine for out of hours telephone enquiries		
2 MONTHS TO GO		- Consider small corporate gift and/or free samples for giving away at event - Produce a strong and relevant icebreaker to start the event - Write second draft of event programme – proof read	- Send out second letters to existing clients - Send out second mailshot - Send out second email shot - Send out second newsletter - First advertisements appear	- Acknowledge second wave of bookings - Arrange small corporate gift and/or free samples. e.g. a diary or pen inscribed with your company contact details - Complete your presentation (including visuals) and start rehearsing - Agree menus and timings with venues. Write to confirm - Advise all speakers that rehearsals will be held the day before the event - Arrange printing of event programme		

	PLANNING	INITIAL PREPARATION	PROMOTION	FINAL PREPARATION	PERFORMANCE	POST PERFORMANCE
1 MONTH TO GO			- Advertisements appear every week 'early right' position. Be prepared for most responses in the second week - Send acknowledgement letter to everyone who has booked - Telephone as many people as possible who have not responded - Send personal invitations to professional introducers and potential introducers to 'top up' numbers	- Prize for card draw - Write to venues to confirm arrangements again, including table and seating layout - Decide what to wear. Take advice! - Arrange licences for playing copyright music - Decide on other attendees from your company and roles - Ensure promotional sales items and stand/banners will be ready - Rehearse your presentation with colleagues and family. Adapt and change it accordingly - Meet other speakers to critique all presentations - Check for interesting anniversaries on the same date as event for any humorous relevance - Write your introduction (for someone else to read) - Prepare a feedback/ evaluation sheet for giving out at event. It should ask attendees if they would have liked information on anything else that was not covered on the day - Prepare updated webpages for uploading on day of event (for attendees only)		

	PLANNING	INITIAL PREPARATION	PROMOTION	FINAL PREPARATION	PERFORMANCE	POST PERFORMANCE
5 DAYS TO GO			- Contact news desk at local radio station - Advise local press of the event. Ask if they want to send a reporter/photographer - Pick up promotional sales material	- Finalise and print seminar handouts - Print and bind any written material for sale if DIY - Check suit is clean - Purchase a new shirt and (red) tie - Purchase new flip chart and pens - Purchase paper, pads, pens etc for attendees - Purchase laser pointer - Ensure leaflet/brochures are collected - Rehearse presentation again - Ensure all other helpers know their roles and finalise timings with them - Prepare a letter that will go to all attendees on the day of the seminar, thanking them for coming along		
4 DAYS TO GO			- Final email to any waverers - Personal telephone call to invite professional introducers who have not responded	- Rehearse presentation		
3 DAYS TO GO				- Rehearse presentation three times		

	PLANNING	INITIAL PREPARATION	PROMOTION	FINAL PREPARATION	PERFORMANCE	POST PERFORMANCE
2 DAYS TO GO			- Telephone or email as many attendees as possible to say looking forward to seeing them	- Rehearse presentation again		
1 DAY TO GO				- Visit venue to final check arrangements - Take all materials, including handouts and free samples - Take your diary to the venue - Set up the room and promotional stand - Ideally stay overnight - Final rehearsals if possible with all speakers - Do not rehearse your presentation after the dress rehearsals		
THE SEMINAR			- Put up promotional banners in visible location at hotel - Locate staff near hotel entrance to meet and direct. Show - don't point!		- Have a light breakfast, ideally with fruit. No coffee or tea. Drink water and/or fruit juice - Do not rehearse your presentation, but do warm up your brain (e.g. times tables, read newspaper) - Scan newspaper for any topical issues - Get access to the room ideally 2 hours in advance to check everything is in place - Turn on all technology and check presentation works - Put an introductory slide on the screen	

	PLANNING	INITIAL PREPARATION	PROMOTION	FINAL PREPARATION	PERFORMANCE	POST PERFORMANCE
					- Ask hotel for piped music unless using own with appropriate licences - Practise speaking from the lectern as though the room is full - Visualise the audience at the end of the seminar. Visualise a group of people that are smiling, content and keen to meet you - Meet and greet as many attendees as possible. Introduce yourself as the event host. Give them a business card when you meet them - Make sure that a register is taken of every attendee - Give each attendee a small corporate gift. e.g. a diary or pen inscribed with your company name, web address and telephone number - Point out business card draw. If people don't have one, give them a blank sheet of card to complete - Make sure there's space for their email address - Enjoy! - Point out that you will be available to take further questions afterwards	

IMMEDIATELY AFTERWARDS	PLANNING	INITIAL PREPARATION	PROMOTION	FINAL PREPARATION	PERFORMANCE	POST PERFORMANCE
						Ask for completion of the feedback sheet - Thank as many attendees as possible - Sell any products - Make any appointments requested - Have a stiff drink – you've done really well

	PLANNING	INITIAL PREPARATION	PROMOTION	FINAL PREPARATION	PERFORMANCE	POST PERFORMANCE
LATER THAT DAY						- Send out previously prepared thank you letters to all attendees. Add handwritten comments as appropriate to reflect anything interesting that happened or was said during the event - Find answers to any questions that could not be answered and telephone the questioner - Put a date in the diary for your next one-off seminar
THE NEXT DAY						- Finish sending out any immediate follow-ups not yet completed - Contact anyone that you are aware of who did not attend - Analyse feedback sheets and take note for next time - Hold business card draw and personally deliver the prize - Send a press release to local papers about the day if press did not attend. Include a photo and make reference to its success and plans for future events
ONE WEEK LATER	- Start planning for next one-off seminar					- Start following up attendees with telephone calls - Arrange meetings

Index